At the beginning of the Second World War, the Luftwaffe dominated the skies over Western Europe – its highly trained pilots flying some of the most advanced fighter aircraft yet built.

It was instrumental in achieving some of the Nazis' greatest victories during the early months of the conflict yet it met its match when faced with the outstanding courage and tenacity of British and Commonwealth pilots during the Battle of Britain.

As the war progressed, the Luftwaffe found itself fighting above the frozen wastes of the Soviet Union in winter and above the blistering deserts of North Africa in summer. It was provided with ever more advanced aircraft yet its might was steadily worn away by ceaseless fighting on multiple fronts.

When waves of RAF bombers began a campaign of night raids over occupied Europe and Germany itself, yet another front opened up. The Luftwaffe's night fighters hunted their targets in the dark and the bomber crews sought to evade them. A desperate struggle for supremacy in radar and electronic technology took place as casualties mounted on both side

Towards the end of the war, advances rocket technology gave the Luftwaffe a by then its fate was sealed.

Today it remains difficult to reconcile the s courage of the Luftwaffe's pilots in combat with the poisonous ideology of the regime for which they fought, yet the statistics tell their own story.

German day and night fighter pilots claimed around 70,000 aerial victories during the war, 25,000 British or American aircraft and 45,000 Russian. There were 103 German fighter pilots who shot down more than 100 Allied aircraft each and some 2500 German fighter pilots who reached 'ace' status by shooting down at least five aircraft. Combat losses, however, totalled 40,000, including 21,452 fighters.

Luftwaffe Fighters examines the fighter aircraft flown by the German air force during that time and presents detailed illustrations of notable individual machines.

Dan Sharp

ABOUT CLAES SUNDIN

Illustrator and author Claes was born in 1957 and lives in the southern part of Sweden. Since finishing four years of studies at the University of Uppsala, he has been active as a teacher, marketer, photographer and art director, among other occupations.

Since childhood, Claes has had a strong interest in everything concerning the combat aircraft of the Second World War and later. This interest stems from the time when he, as a boy of seven, started building and collecting plastic scale models. Simultaneously, he has been a keen draftsman for as long as he can remember, as well as an accomplished CGI artist in more recent years. At present, Claes is producing books, writing articles and lecturing. Up to now he has produced more than 2000 CGI profiles, mostly of aircraft, but also of Second World War armour.

His previously published books include: Luftwaffe Fighter Aircraft in Profile (1997), Deutsche Jagdflugzeuge (1998), More Luftwaffe Fighter Aircraft in Profile (2002), Luftwaffe Fighter Aircraft, Limited Edition (2011), Luftwaffe Fighter Aircraft, Profile Book No 1 (2013), Allied Fighter Aircraft, Profile Book No

2 (2013), Tiger and Panther Tanks (2014), Luftwaffe Fighter Aircraft, Profile Book No 3 (2014), and Luftwaffe Attack Aircraft, Profile Book No 4 (2015) and Profiles of German Tanks (2015). In addition, he has provided aircraft and tank profiles, photo refinement, and artwork for many other books and papers.

Claes says: "As a long time profile artist, I am well aware that a few of the profiles included in this publication will be the subject of some criticism. The reader however, must acknowledge that all the profiles included are based on solid photographic documentation. I will always use at least one reference photo, more if available, of the subject. I seek the best photos available for the related close-up details as well.

"However, misinterpretations could naturally occur, especially regarding the colours I've chosen for the different profiles. One has to appreciate the difficulty of interpreting the colours from dated black and white photographs. But know that I have, together with my colleagues, made the utmost effort to determine the actual appearance and colouring of the individual aircraft profiles presented here."

LUFTWAFFE FIGHTERS | CONTENTS

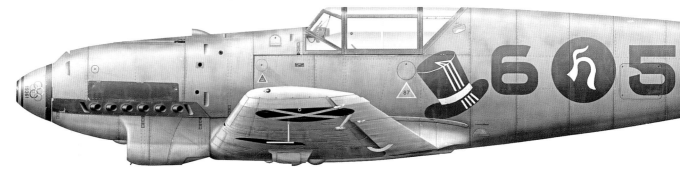

6 | MESSERSCHMITT BF 109

062 | FOCKE-WULF FW 190/TA 152

108 | DORNIER DO 17/215/217

116 | MESSERSCHMITT ME 163

All illustrations:
CLAES SUNDIN

Design:
ATG-MEDIA.COM

Publishing director:
DAN SAVAGE

Publisher:
STEVE O'HARA

Reprographics:
JONATHAN SCHOFIELD & PAUL FINCHAM

Production editor:
DAN SHARP

Marketing manager:
CHARLOTTE PARK

Commercial director:
NIGEL HOLE

Published by:
MORTONS MEDIA GROUP LTD, MEDIA CENTRE, MORTON WAY, HORNCASTLE, LINCOLNSHIRE LN9 6JR.

Tel. 01507 529529

MORTONS MEDIA GROUP LTD

Printed by: **WILLIAM GIBBONS AND SONS, WOLVERHAMPTON**

ISBN: 978-1-911276-25-8

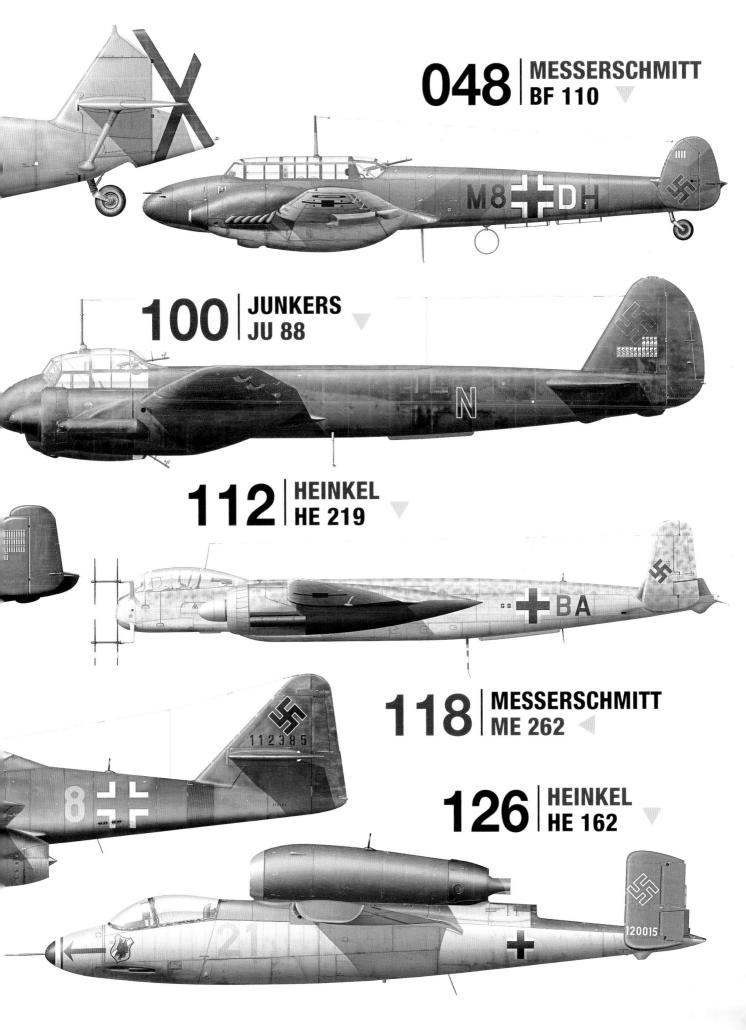

048 | MESSERSCHMITT BF 110 ▼

100 | JUNKERS JU 88 ▼

112 | HEINKEL HE 219 ▼

118 | MESSERSCHMITT ME 262 ◄

126 | HEINKEL HE 162 ▼

130 | COLOUR CHART

BF 109 C-1

Hauptmann Gotthard Handrick of Condor Legion fighter group 2.J/88 flew 6-56 during the Spanish Civil War, based at Estracón, Spain. Handrick, a gold medal-winning athlete at the 1936 Olympics, shot down a Polikarpov I-16 on May 18, 1938.

BF 109 E-3

The personal aircraft of Oberleutnant Hans 'Schmolly' von Schmoller-Haldy of 3.J/88, based at Tarragona, Spain, in March 1939 was 6-123. The beer mug, his personal emblem, bears the initials 'CP' in reference to an international pilots' drinking club in Belgium known as Cardinal Paff.

MESSERSCHMITT
BF 109

1935-1945

It is difficult to exaggerate the importance of the legendary Messerschmitt Bf 109 to the Luftwaffe during the Second World War. Small, lightweight and fast, the single-seater was continually upgraded and remained at the cutting edge of piston-engined fighter technology right up to the bitter end. Flown by all of the Luftwaffe's most prolific aces, it has become an iconic symbol of German aerial prowess. Today it remains one of the world's most recognisable aircraft.

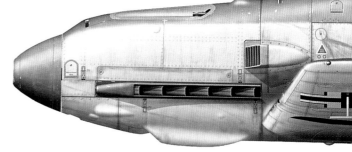

The story of the Bf 109 began with the founding of a new aircraft company in Augsburg in 1926 – Bayerische Flugzeugwerke AG. This firm was forged from the remnants of another company, Udet Flugzeugbau, which had collapsed only months earlier. Young aircraft designer Willy Messerschmitt was appointed as the firm's chief designer in 1927 and a string of successful lightweight sports and commercial aircraft followed.

In July 1933, Bayerische Flugzeugwerke was invited to tender for a new RLM requirement. This called for a single-seat day fighter armed with two fixed forward-firing machine guns, radio gear enabling air-to-air and ground-to-air communications and pilot equipment including a harness, oxygen system and heating with room for a parachute. The fighter would have to maintain a speed of 400kph for up to 20 minutes at 6000m, remain aloft for an hour, reach that altitude in 17 minutes and have a service ceiling of 10,000m.

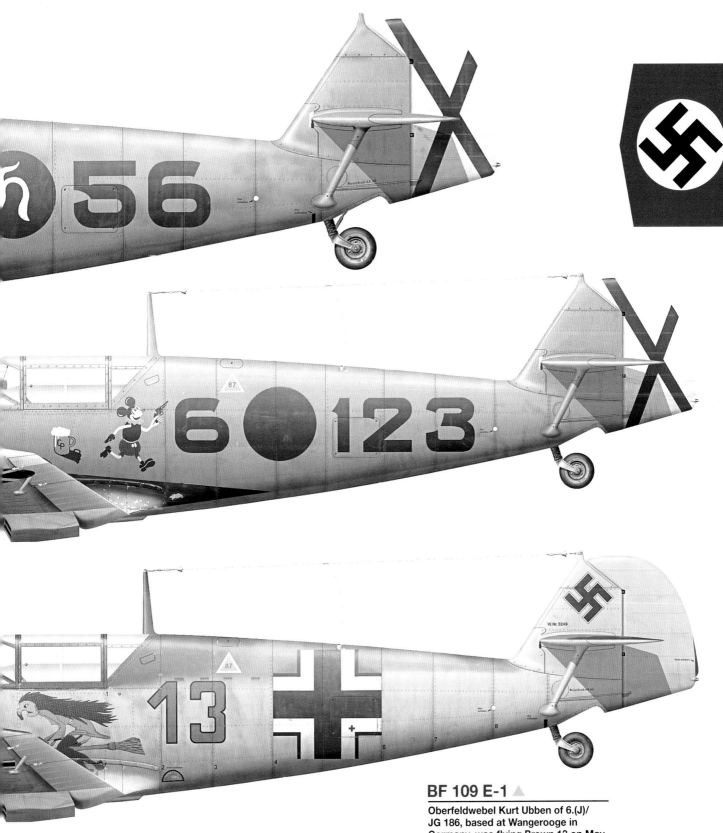

BF 109 E-1

Oberfeldwebel Kurt Ubben of 6.(J)/ JG 186, based at Wangerooge in Germany, was flying Brown 13 on May 10, 1940, when he shot down a Dutch Fokker D.XXI fighter over Holland.

It also had to be suitable for pilots of average ability, easy to recover from a spin, capable of flying in fog and cloud, be small enough to transport by rail, have protection against leakage of fuel and be able to land on an airfield of 400m by 400m with a 400m approach.

Range was not mentioned, nor was any further requirement for additional armament or load carrying ability. The winning design would be the aircraft that replaced Germany's then-standard Arado Ar 64 and Heinkel He 51 fighters.

Messerschmitt set to work on an aircraft that would meet these conditions but then, in September 1933, Bayerische Flugzeugwerke was contracted to build a new four-seater all-metal aircraft to participate in the 4th Challenge International de Tourisme competition in 1934.

Messerschmitt's M 23 design had already won it twice, in 1929 and 1930, and Bayerische Flugzeugwerke naturally took the job. Messerschmitt applied some of the ideas he had been working on for the fighter project

to the design and the result was the very modern-looking M 37 low-wing monoplane.

Even before this made its first flight, the firm submitted its fighter design to the RLM and received a development contract for it in February 1934. Even as the M 37 made its first flight, detail design work was already commencing on the new fighter.

Powered by a 247hp Hirth HM 8U inverted V engine and now

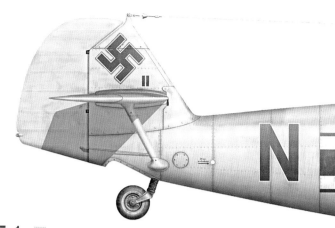

under the official designation Bf 108, the sports aircraft was flown by four of the 13 German participants in a field of 34 competitors during late August and early September 1934 – the others flying Fieseler Fi 97s and Klemm Kl 36s. Defeated overall by Polish teams flying RWD 9s, the Bf 108 nevertheless took the top three places in both the maximum speed and fuel consumption trials.

The design was a success and orders began to roll in. But while the Bf 108 was enjoying very public success, Bayerische Flugzeugwerke's new fighter was taking shape behind closed doors. A mock-up was inspected in January 1935 and the type received the RLM designation Bf 109.

Its competitors were Arado's Ar 80, the Heinkel He 112 and latterly the Focke-Wulf Fw 159.

BF 109 E-1

Black 4 was flown by Oberfeldwebel Anton 'Toni' Hackl of 5./JG 77, based at Kristiansand-Kjevik, Norway, during late June 1940. On June 15, he shot down two RAF Lockheed Hudsons, then he destroyed a Handley Page Hereford on June 21 and then another Hudson on June 27.

The Ar 80 suffered from an overly complex landing gear retraction system, resulting in its gear eventually being fixed in place. It also had an open cockpit and performed poorly. Similarly, the Fw 159 had gear problems and its parasol wing arrangement made it look fragile and old fashioned.

The He 112, however, was the Bf 109's real competition. It had a sturdy wide-track retractable undercarriage, low-set gullwings and an enclosed cockpit. With the Ar 80 and Fw 159 eliminated early on, the He 112 went head-to-head with the Bf 109 and was initially the favourite of the two to win.

It could out-turn the Bf 109 due to its larger wings but the Bf 109 was faster at any altitude, more

BF 109 E-4

Oberleutnant Werner Machold of 9./JG 2, based at Le Havre-Octeville, flew Brown 5 and shot down nine RAF aircraft during September 1940. On June 9, 1941, he force-landed near Swanage, Dorset, and became a PoW for the rest of the war.

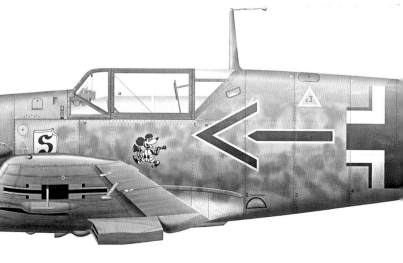

BF 109 D-1

The first RAF Bomber Command aircraft to be shot down during the Second World War was a 49 Squadron Handley Page Hampden on the night of April 26/27. The fighter responsible was Black N+7, flown by Oberfeldwebel Hermann Förster of 11.(N)/JG 2, based at Oslo-Fornebu, Norway.

agile and able to perform aerobatic manoeuvres much more easily. The contest had begun on February 8, 1936, and less than a month later, on March 2, the Bf 109 V2 and He 112 V2 were to perform spin tests. The Bf 109 V2 was able to spin and recover with ease – but the He 112 V2 was not, and crashed. The following month, after repairs, the latter was flown again but crashed again and this time was damaged beyond repair.

On March 12, the RLM produced a policy document indicating that the Bf 109 was the preferred design but nevertheless a series of 10 pre-production aircraft were ordered from each company. Four He 112s in different configurations had been tested by the end of September 1936

THE BF 109 WAS FASTER AND MORE AGILE THAN ITS COMPETITOR THE HE 112

BF 109 E-4

Before his promotion to high command, Adolf Galland was a front line fighter pilot. He was flying this aircraft, Chevron Bar, with Stab/JG 26, from Audembert, France, on September 24, 1940, when he shot down a Hawker Hurricane – possibly P3878 flown by HAC Bird-Wilson of 17 Squadron.

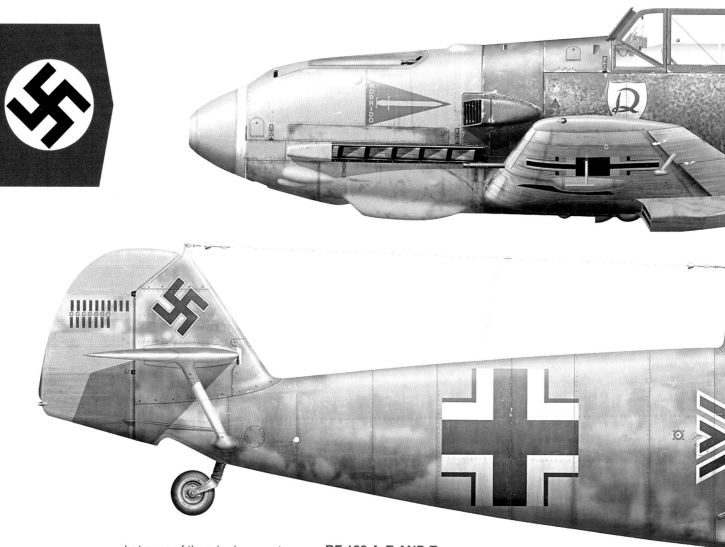

BF 109 A-E AND T

but none of them had proven to be a match for the Bf 109s.

Ultimately, the He 112 was let down by its heavier and less aerodynamic design and the Bf 109 went on to become the Luftwaffe's standard fighter. It was a mistake that Heinkel was determine to undo – prompting him to commission the He 100 which would briefly hold the world air speed record in 1939. The search for a truly clean aerodynamic layout would continue to inform Heinkel's designs throughout the Second World War.

The Bf 109 V1, powered by a Rolls-Royce Kestrel VI, was used for the design competition, as were the V2 and V3, each fitted with Jumo 210 A engine. The latter two were sent to Spain for operational evaluation during November 1936 but neither saw any action and neither did the seven pre-production Bf 109 As that were built shortly thereafter.

They were used to test a variety of configurations including different engines, various cockpit and gun ventilation apertures and numerous oil cooler alterations. Each was armed with just a pair of engine cowling-mounted MG 17 7.92mm machine guns.

The first Bf 109 B was the first version to see action – being sent to serve with the Condor Legion during the

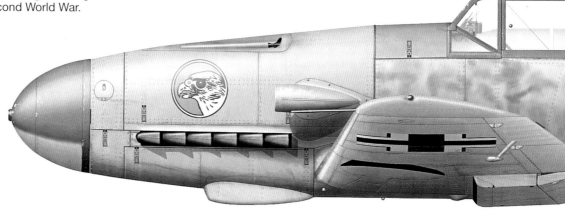

BF 109 E-4

Hauptmann Helmut Wick of Stab I.JG 2, based at Mardyck in Belgium, was flying this aircraft on October 5, 1940, when he shot down three Hurricanes over Bournemouth, then two Spitfires over the Isle of Wight.

BF 109 E-4

Double Chevron flown by Hauptmann Rolf Pingel of Stab I./JG 26, based at St Omer-Claimairais, France, during December 1940. Pingel had 23 victories by this point.

BF 109 F-1

Oberstleutnant Werner Mölders of Stab./ JG 51, based at Mardyck, France, shot down a Spitfire on May 8, 1941, while flying this aircraft – his 82nd victory of the war.

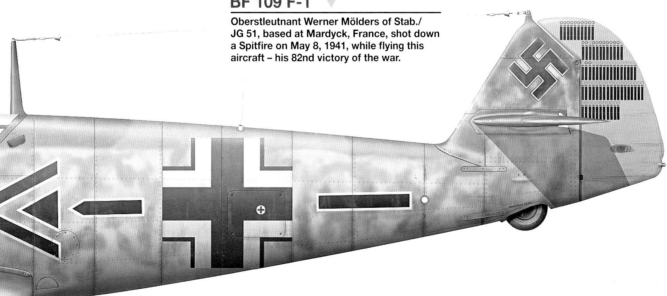

MESSERSCHMITT BF 109

BF 109 F-2

The aircraft flown by Stab II./JG 53's Hauptmann Heinz Bretnütz during May 1941, while the unit was still based at St Omer-Arques in France. Bretnütz led II./JG 53 during the invasion of Russia but was badly injured on June 22 and died after having his leg amputated.

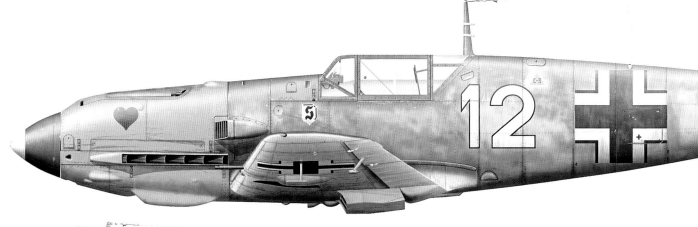

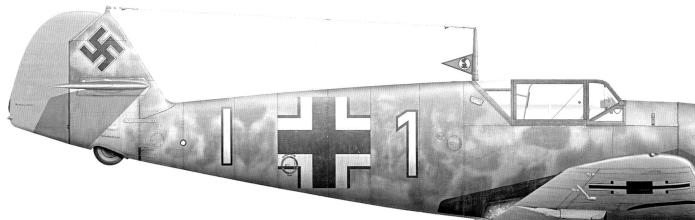

BF 109 F-2

Some of Oberleutnant Egon Mayer's earliest aerial victories were won in June 1941 while flying White 1 with 7./JG 2 from Thèville in France.

BF 109 E-4/B

Yellow F of 6.(Schl.)/LG 2, at Praschnitz, Poland, on June 22, 1941.

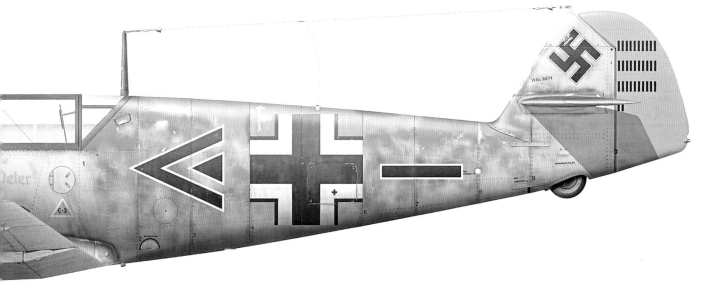

BF 109 E-7

White 12, flown by Oberleutnant Joachim Müncheberg of 7./JG 26, based at Ain El Gazala in Libya during June 1941.

Spanish Civil War in 1937. It was powered by a Jumo 210 D but still only armed with a pair of MG 17s. Three firms produced the Bf 109 B – Messerschmitt itself, Fieseler and Erla.

Production of the next variant, the Bf 109 C, began during the spring of 1938. It featured a new oil system with a larger capacity tank and strengthened wings that could now carry another MG 17 each, for a total of four including those mounted on the engine cowling. The biggest change, however, was a newly upgraded engine – the Jumo 210 G which produced 690hp and boasted direct fuel injection.

Minor detail changes included larger exhausts, improved instrumentation, a reduced windscreen angle, the external electrical socket being moved from below the cockpit sill on the starboard side to fuselage frame 2 and the oxygen filler point being relocated aft of the cockpit on the starboard side.

Just 58 Bf 109 Cs were made.

The Bf 109 D was based on the C but with the Jumo 210 D from the Bf 109 B fitted instead of the Jumo 210 G. The D-1 became the Luftwaffe's standard fighter just before the beginning of the Second World War and 657 were made, all but four of them by subcontractors AGO, Arado, Erla, Fieseler and Focke-Wulf.

All these early types had been just a precursor of what was to come however. The first Bf 109 to be made in truly astonishing numbers and a wide variety of sub-types was the Bf 109 E, entering production in late 1938. Again, the biggest change was a new engine – this time the Jumo 210 being replaced entirely by the much more powerful Daimler-Benz DB 601 A. It was longer and 400lb heavier but it gave the Bf 109 a respectable 1085hp, compared to the Jumo 210's 690hp.

Rather than enlarge the existing nose-mounted radiator to provide the necessary cooling for this

THE FIRST BF 109 TO BE MADE IN TRULY ASTONISHING NUMBERS AND A WIDE VARIETY OF SUB-TYPES WAS THE BF 109 E

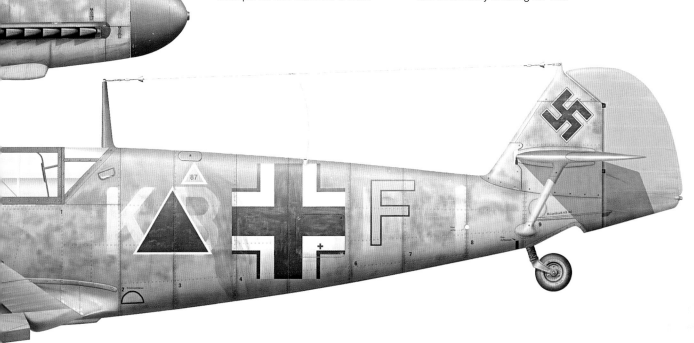

MESSERSCHMITT BF 109

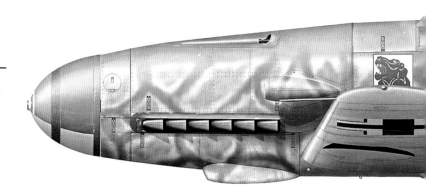

BF 109 F-2 ▶

Double Chevron flown by Hauptmann
Dietrich Hrabak of Stab II./JG 54 from
Ostrow in the USSR, July 30, 1941.

BF 109 E-7 TROP ▼

Feldwebel Günther Steinhausen
of 1./JG 27 flew White 10 from
Ain-El-Gazala, Libya, during
August 1941. He shot down two
Hurricanes of 1 Squadron SAAF
on August 2 and then a P-40
flown by Sergeant M S Hards of
250 Squadron RAF on August 26.

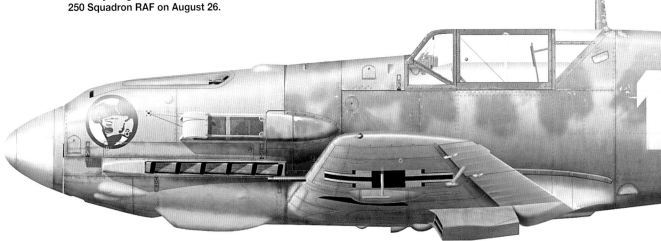

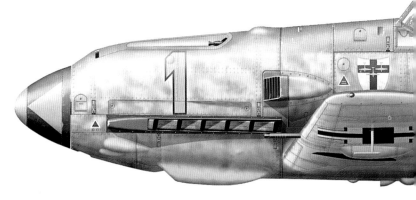

new power plant, Messerschmitt
instead moved the main radiators
to the underside of its wings. The
oil cooler that was positioned
under the nose appears as little
more than a streamlined slot.

Putting the radiators under the
wings meant they had to be almost
completely redesigned to cope
with the weight but this also served
to provide a counterbalance
to the weight of the engine.
The aircraft's armament,
however, remained the same.

After an initial batch of 10
pre-production E-0s, the E-1
production version was ordered
and 1183 were built. The E-2
kept the usual cowling MG 17s
but supplemented them with a
single MG FF 20mm autocannon
mounted in the engine that could
fire through the aircraft's spinner
and two more MG FFs in the
wings. This combination did
not work as well as expected,
however, and only a small number
of E-2s were made. Instead,
production switched to the
E-3 which deleted the engine

cannon but kept the other two.
The various subcontractors
turned out 1276 examples.

At the beginning of the Battle
of Britain during the summer of
1940, the E-3 was in the process
of being replaced by the E-4 – with
many E-3s being updated to E-4
standard. This meant swapping
the MG FFs for improved MG
FF/Ms and providing the pilot

with better armour protection
for his head. A new cockpit
canopy was introduced too,
offering a wider field of vision.

The production run went to 496
E-4s, with some 65 E-3s being
upgraded. Later examples were
fitted with the 1159hp DB 601 N
engine, designed for high altitude
work. Both the E-5 and E-6 were
reconnaissance platforms based

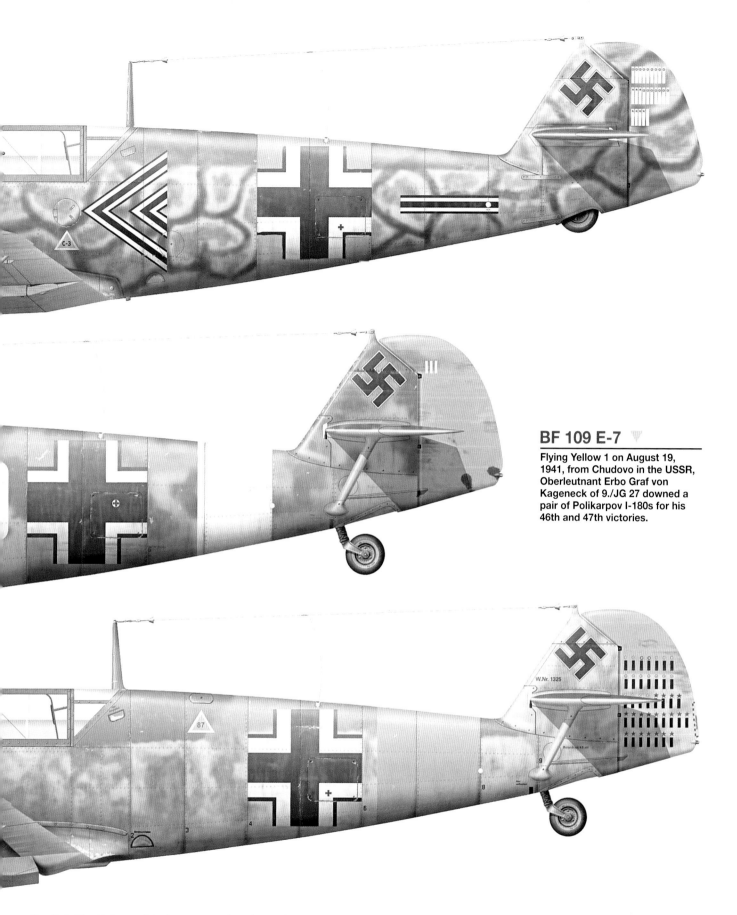

BF 109 E-7

Flying Yellow 1 on August 19, 1941, from Chudovo in the USSR, Oberleutnant Erbo Graf von Kageneck of 9./JG 27 downed a pair of Polikarpov I-180s for his 46th and 47th victories.

on the E-1. The E-5 was fitted with a Zeiss Rb 21/18 camera in its fuselage behind the cockpit, while the E-6 had the smaller Rb 12,5/7 x 9. Just 29 of the former were made and nine of the latter.

The E-7 was intended to address the horrendously limited range of the earlier versions – the Bf 109 having been originally envisioned as an interceptor rather than a long-range fighter. It was the first Bf 109 able to carry a drop tank, specifically the Luftwaffe's standard 300 litre unit mounted on a rack under the centreline of the fuselage, and range was consequently increased from 410 miles to 820 miles.

The same rack could, alternatively, be used to carry a bomb – making the E-7 a fighter-bomber of sorts. With the introduction of the E-7 at the end of August 1940, a programme of upgrades was begun to bring all other Bf 109s in service up to the same standard. A total of 438 purpose-built Bf 109 E-7s were made.

One final Bf 109 E was produced, the E-8, but these were created by modifying existing

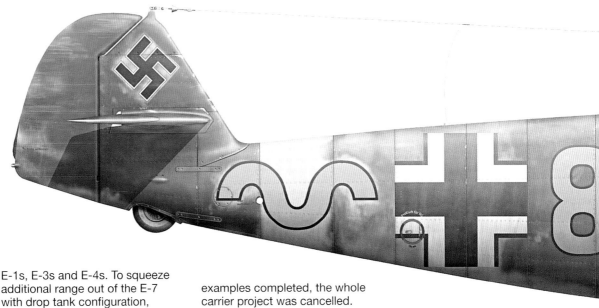

AS THE BATTLE OF BRITAIN ENTERED ITS FINAL STAGE THE LUFTWAFFE BEGAN TO RECEIVE DELIVERIES OF THE NEXT MAJOR REVISION OF THE BF 109 - THE F

E-1s, E-3s and E-4s. To squeeze additional range out of the E-7 with drop tank configuration, armament was downgraded to just four MG 17s – which were substantially lighter than MG FFs.

Overall, more than 3400 Bf 109 Es were made. On top of these were 70 Bf 109 Ts. Before the war, the Germans had set out plans to construct a fleet of four aircraft carriers and although this was subsequently reduced to just two, it was still necessary to produce specialised aircraft for them – specifically navalised Bf 109s and Ju 87s. The 'T' in Bf 109 T stood for Träger or 'carrier'.

The type, based on the Bf 109 E-7, did not require folding wings, since the lifts on the German carriers would be designed to accommodate its increased 11.8m wingspan, but it did need an arrester hook and catapult fixings. An initial production batch of 70 Bf 109 T-1s was ordered from Fieseler but with only seven examples completed, the whole carrier project was cancelled.

The remaining 63 were built as the T-2, retaining the 11.8m wings but without the hooks and the other naval gear. They were assigned to I/JG 77 and proved useful in Norway where their longer wings made landing and taking off in strong crosswinds easier.

BF 109 F
As the Battle of Britain entered its final stage, during September 1940, the Luftwaffe began to receive deliveries of the next major revision of the Bf 109 – the F. Having been in development since 1939, this was an improvement on the E in almost every respect. Wing mounted weaponry was deleted entirely in favour of a single engine-mounted MG FF/M 20mm cannon and the two cowling MG 17s.

BF 109 F-2 ▽
Major Hannes Trautloft, flew this aircraft with Stab./JG 54 from Siverskaya, Russia, during February 1942 when his tally stood at 31 victories.

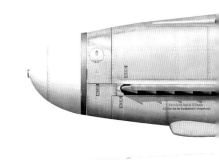

BF 109 F-4 TROP ▲
During a 10 minute engagement on February 15, 1942, Oberfeldwebel Otto Schulz of 4./JG 27, based at Martuba, Libya, shot down five RAF Curtiss P-40 Kittyhawks – one of them flown by British ace Squadron Leader Ernest 'Imshi' Mason of 94 Squadron, who was killed.

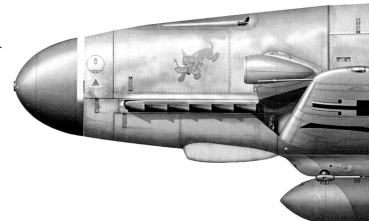

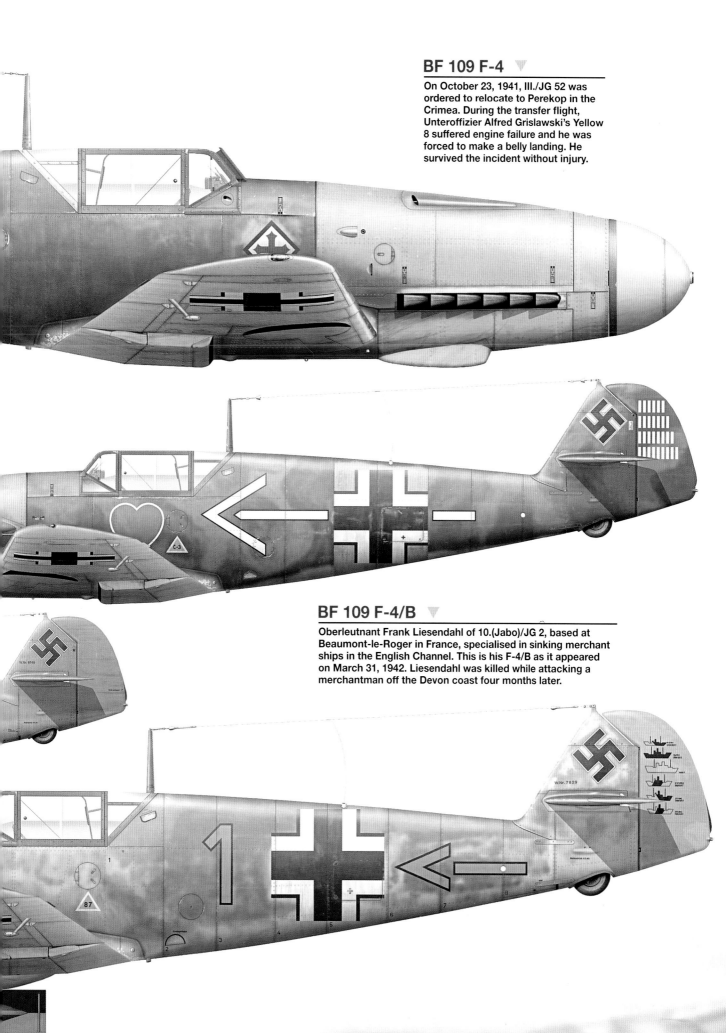

BF 109 F-4 ▼

On October 23, 1941, III./JG 52 was ordered to relocate to Perekop in the Crimea. During the transfer flight, Unteroffizier Alfred Grislawski's Yellow 8 suffered engine failure and he was forced to make a belly landing. He survived the incident without injury.

BF 109 F-4/B ▼

Oberleutnant Frank Liesendahl of 10.(Jabo)/JG 2, based at Beaumont-le-Roger in France, specialised in sinking merchant ships in the English Channel. This is his F-4/B as it appeared on March 31, 1942. Liesendahl was killed while attacking a merchantman off the Devon coast four months later.

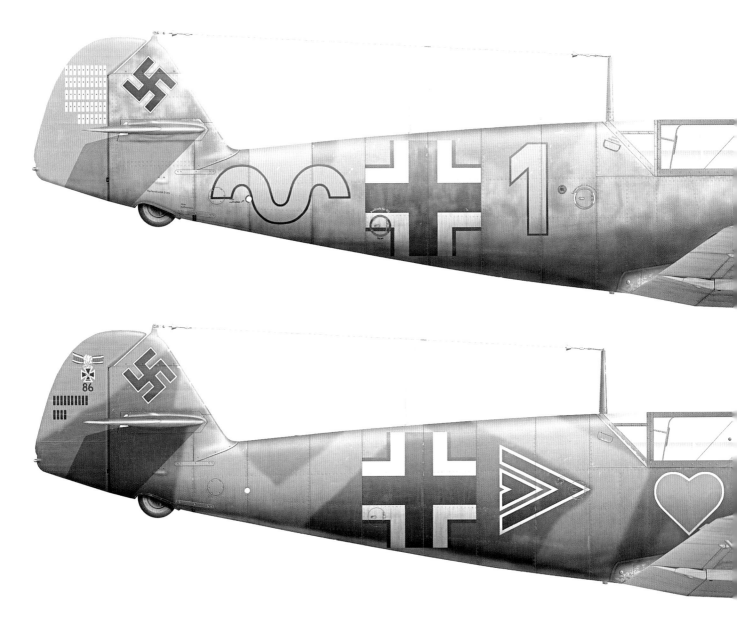

BF 109 F-4

Shooting down an Il-2 Sturmovik and a MiG-1 while flying White 4 was just another day at the office for Feldwebel Hans Schleef of 7./JG 3, based at Tschugujew in the USSR on May 22, 1942. Between February and September that year he accounted for 72 Soviet aircraft.

BF 109 F-4

Leutnant Hermann Graf of 9./JG 52, based at Kharkov-Rogan in the USSR, flew Yellow 1 during late March 1942. On March 23 he shot down two Yak-1s and an Su-2, on the 25th he got another Yak-1, then another on the 27th along with a MiG-3. On the 28th he destroyed two I-16s, another Yak-1 and another MiG-3, and on the 30th he got another I-16.

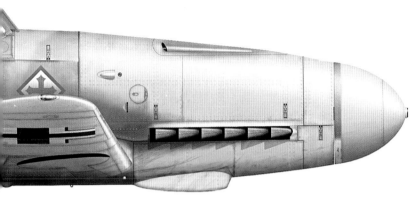

BF 109 F-2

On March 31, 1942, Hauptmann Hans Philipp became only the fourth Luftwaffe pilot to achieve 100 victories. He was flying this aircraft with Stab I./JG 54.

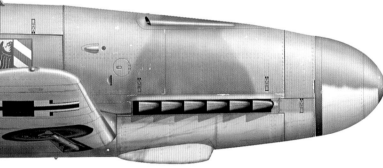

The engine cowling was redesigned to become more aerodynamically efficient and the propeller spinner was enlarged to blend smoothly into the cowling.

Armour protection for the pilot's head was improved again and his seat was reshaped to be smaller and more figure-hugging, although it also became non-adjustable. A new self-sealing fuel tank was also provided with armour, the hydraulic system was completely redesigned, the radiator flaps became thermostatically controlled and the oil cooler was enlarged. These alterations, particularly the aircraft's more streamlined shape, helped to significantly increase range – up to 1060 miles with a light alloy drop tank.

Other alternations included a slight reduction in rudder area, the horizontal tailplanes were repositioned slightly down and forward and lost their bracing struts, the tailwheel became semi-retractable and the undercarriage mainwheel legs were angled forward by six degrees with the aim of improving handling while taxiing. The whole tail structure was also reinforced.

The Bf 109 F also featured completely redesigned wings, with the tip shape being changed and their overall area being reduced slightly. New shorter, thicker leading edge slats were fitted and the underwing radiators became less prominent and were repositioned further to the rear.

It was intended that the Bf 109 F should be powered by

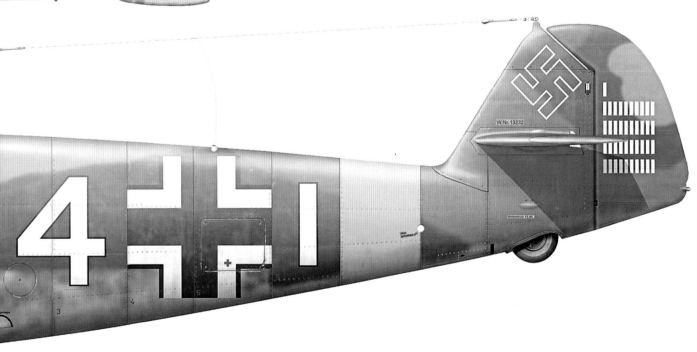

BF 109 F-4 TROP

Yellow 14, flown by Leutnant Hans-Joachim Marseille of 3./JG 27, from Tmimi in Libya on June 1, 1942. A short while later Marseille, a classically trained pianist, was flown back to Germany and required to perform for dignitaries including Hitler, Göring, Goebbels, Arthur Axmann and Erhard Milch. He was killed in action three months later.

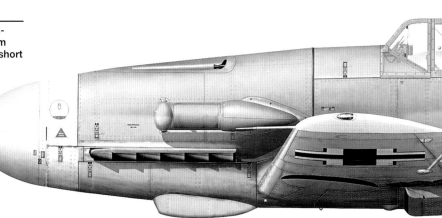

the new DB 601 E but this was initially unavailable so pre-production F-0 machines, plus F-1 and F-2 production machines, received the DB 601 N. Both Messerschmitt itself and Wiener Neustädter Flugzeugwerke (WNF) produced the F-1, with 208 being built all together.

For the F-2, the MG FF/M engine-mounted cannon was replaced by a 15mm Mauser MG 151 cannon – which itself was replaced by the 20mm version of the same gun as it began to become available. From October 1940 to August 1941, AGO, Arado, Erla, Messerschmitt and WNF managed to construct around 1380 F-2s between them.

The F-3 finally saw the introduction of the DB 601 E – though only 15 were made between October 1940 and

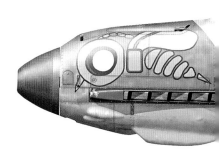

January 1941, all of them by Messerschmitt, and with the same armament as the F-1. The F-4 also had the DB 601 E but had the same armament as the F-2, including its new MG 151 20mm cannon. Production lasted a full year, from May 1941 to May 1942, with 1841 F-4s built – including 544 F-4/Zs, which had a GM-1 boost feature added for high-altitude operations, and 576 F-4 Trops, which had filters fitted for dusty or sandy environments.

The Bf 109 F was the standard fighter of the Luftwaffe as the invasion of the Soviet Union, Operation Barbarossa, commenced on June 22, 1941.

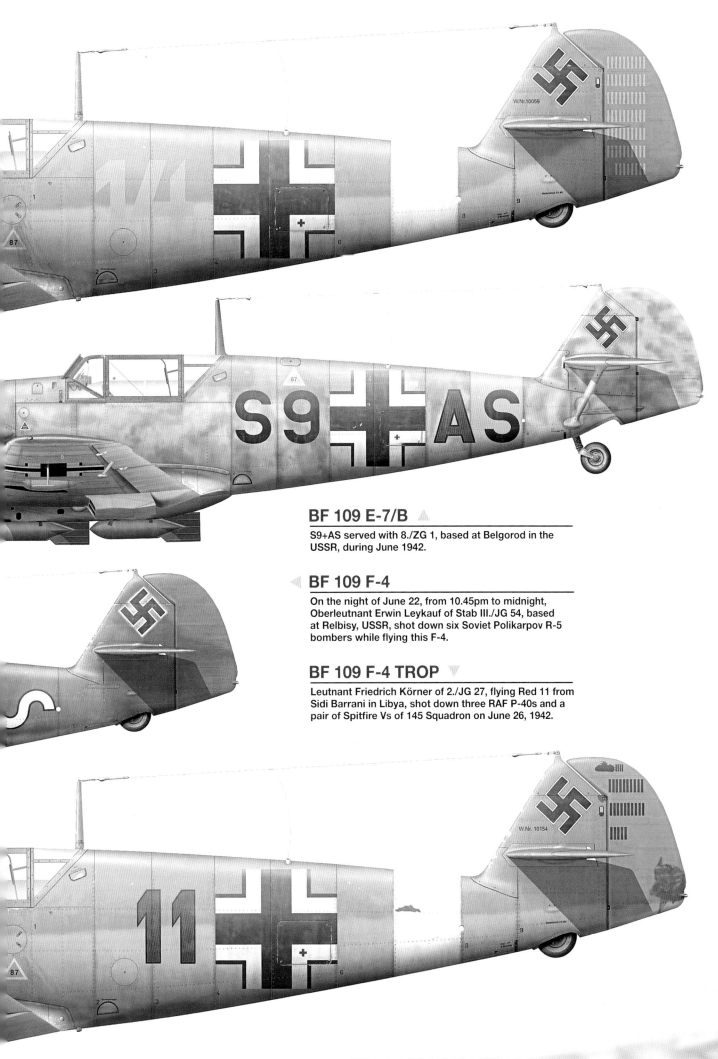

BF 109 E-7/B

S9+AS served with 8./ZG 1, based at Belgorod in the USSR, during June 1942.

BF 109 F-4

On the night of June 22, from 10.45pm to midnight, Oberleutnant Erwin Leykauf of Stab III./JG 54, based at Relbisy, USSR, shot down six Soviet Polikarpov R-5 bombers while flying this F-4.

BF 109 F-4 TROP

Leutnant Friedrich Körner of 2./JG 27, flying Red 11 from Sidi Barrani in Libya, shot down three RAF P-40s and a pair of Spitfire Vs of 145 Squadron on June 26, 1942.

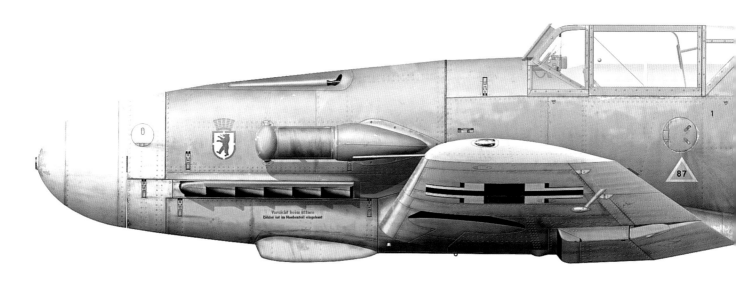

BF 109 F-2

Hauptmann Hans von Hahn of Stab I./JG 3 flew this aircraft from Lutsk in the USSR on July 6, 1942. Hahn's final victory of the war had been 11 months earlier, on August 16, 1941. In June 1942, he had been relieved of his command and confined to quarters after allegedly shooting a sentry. He was subsequently reinstated.

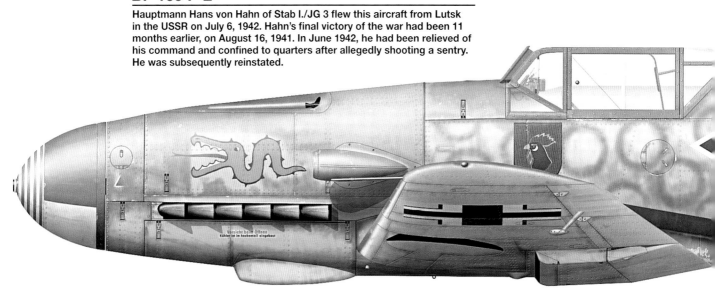

BF 109 F-4

The Staffelkapitän of 1./JG 3, Oberleutnant Helmut 'Pitt' Mertens, downed a Yak-1 west of Stalingrad on August 1, 1942, while flying White 111 – his 50th victory. The unit was based at Frolov in the USSR at the time.

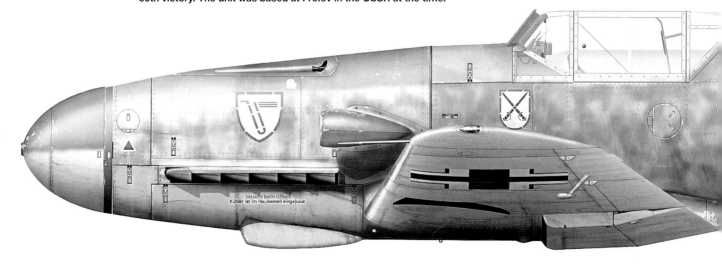

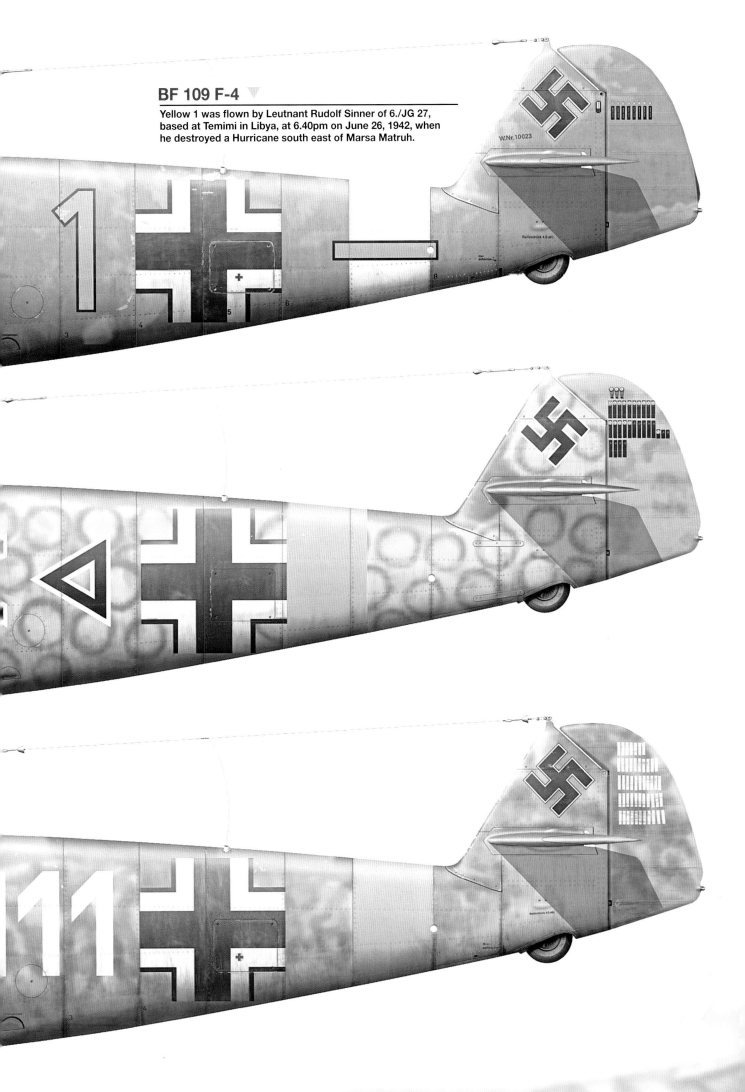

BF 109 F-4

Yellow 1 was flown by Leutnant Rudolf Sinner of 6./JG 27, based at Temimi in Libya, at 6.40pm on June 26, 1942, when he destroyed a Hurricane south east of Marsa Matruh.

W.Nr. 10023

MESSERSCHMITT BF 109

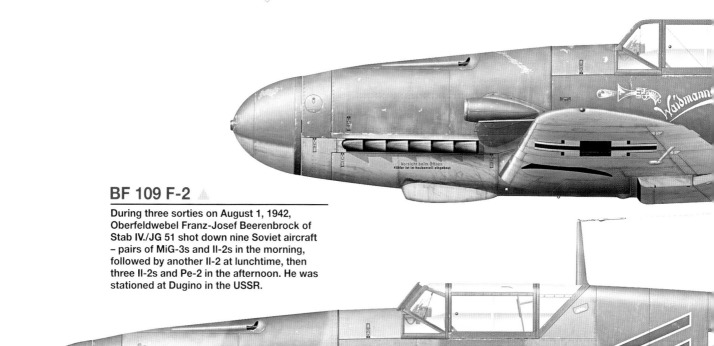

BF 109 F-2

During three sorties on August 1, 1942, Oberfeldwebel Franz-Josef Beerenbrock of Stab IV./JG 51 shot down nine Soviet aircraft – pairs of MiG-3s and Il-2s in the morning, followed by another Il-2 at lunchtime, then three Il-2s and Pe-2 in the afternoon. He was stationed at Dugino in the USSR.

BF 109 G

During February 1942, with the Bf 109 F-4 still in production, Messerschmitt introduced yet another upgrade in the form of the Bf 109 G. Largely based on the F series, the G was developed in response to ever-increasing Allied capabilities and was intended to give the Bf 109 greater flexibility to fulfil a wide variety of different roles. One particular variant, the Bf 109 G-6, would become the most heavily mass produced fighter variant of the Second World War with some 12,000 built. It alone accounted for more than a third of all Bf 109 production.

The Bf 109 G series was powered by the DB 605 – effectively a DB 601 with bored-out cylinders, altered valve timing to increase revs and a more powerful supercharger. It was identical to the DB 601 in size and near-identical in shape but produced 1455hp compared to 1332hp, albeit with an increase in weight from 700kg to 756kg.

Consequently, the earliest Gs were externally very similar to the F but came with a host of further detail changes. The fuel filler point was relocated close to the spine of the fuselage in frame 3 on the left side and a new heavier cockpit

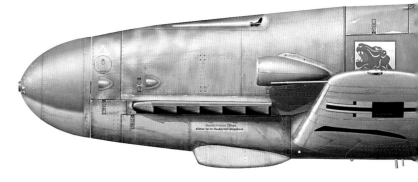

BF 109 G-2

Yellow 4 flown by Leutnant Hans Beisswenger of 6./JG 54 from Dugino in the USSR during August 1942. That month he shot down 23 Yak-1s, five Pe-2s, two Il-2s and a LaGG-3; his overall tally standing at 97 by August 28. He was killed on March 6, 1943, when Yellow 4 was rammed by Soviet ace Starshii Leitenant Ivan Kholodov.

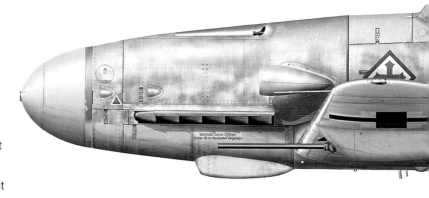

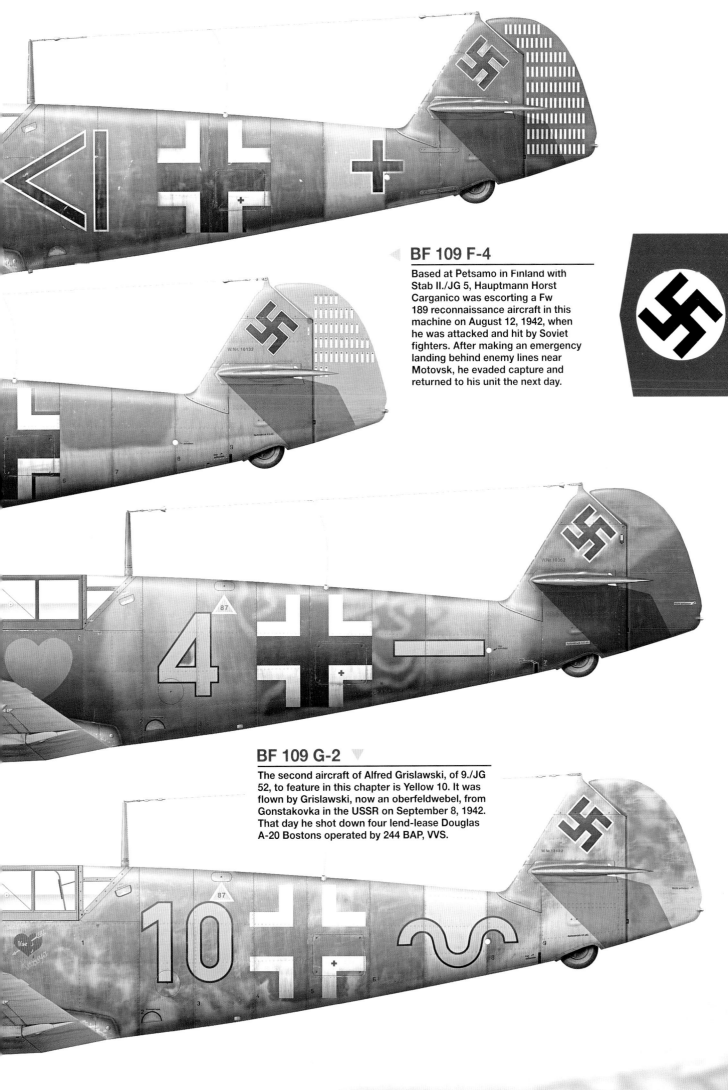

BF 109 F-4

Based at Petsamo in Finland with Stab II./JG 5, Hauptmann Horst Carganico was escorting a Fw 189 reconnaissance aircraft in this machine on August 12, 1942, when he was attacked and hit by Soviet fighters. After making an emergency landing behind enemy lines near Motovsk, he evaded capture and returned to his unit the next day.

BF 109 G-2

The second aircraft of Alfred Grislawski, of 9./JG 52, to feature in this chapter is Yellow 10. It was flown by Grislawski, now an oberfeldwebel, from Gonstakovka in the USSR on September 8, 1942. That day he shot down four lend-lease Douglas A-20 Bostons operated by 244 BAP, VVS.

MESSERSCHMITT BF 109

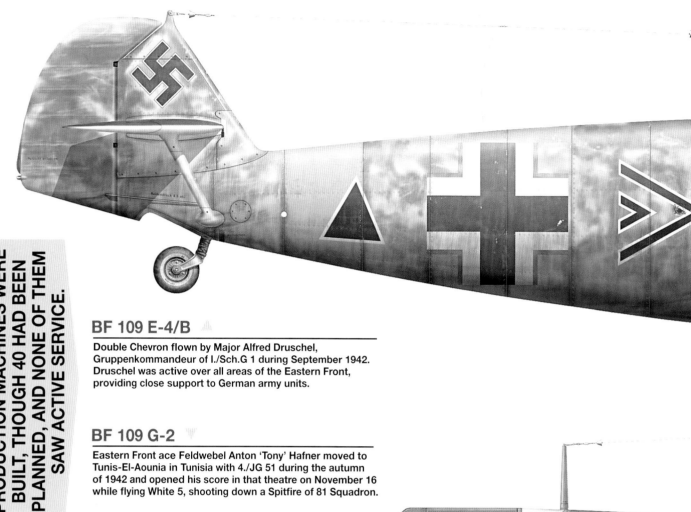

BF 109 E-4/B

Double Chevron flown by Major Alfred Druschel, Gruppenkommandeur of I./Sch.G 1 during September 1942. Druschel was active over all areas of the Eastern Front, providing close support to German army units.

BF 109 G-2

Eastern Front ace Feldwebel Anton 'Tony' Hafner moved to Tunis-El-Aounia in Tunisia with 4./JG 51 during the autumn of 1942 and opened his score in that theatre on November 16 while flying White 5, shooting down a Spitfire of 81 Squadron.

canopy was introduced. This was a welded structure, where the F's canopy had had a light tubular structure, and came with a built-in armour glass windscreen.

A windscreen washer was also introduced in the form of a small tube which ran along the screen and could spray fuel onto the glass to clear away oil or other obstructions. Ventilation

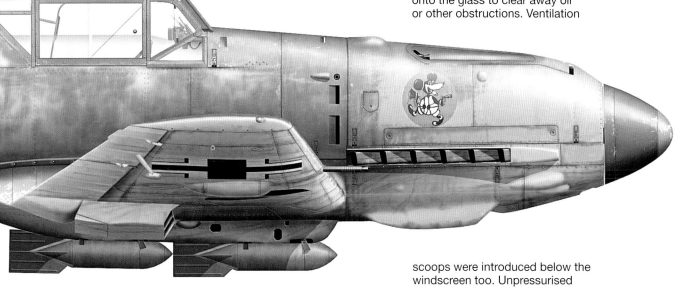

scoops were introduced below the windscreen too. Unpressurised Bf 109 Gs usually also had a rectangular ventilation inlet on either side of the cockpit, although these were sometimes sealed up or omitted altogether.

A deeper oil radiator was now fitted and emergency shut-off valves were installed which would allow the pilot to isolate the wing radiators in the event of a coolant leak – to prevent the vital fluid completely draining away, which would result in near-instantaneous engine seizure. The tailwheel of the G could also be locked in position to make take-offs and landings easier.

Practical operational experience was also applied to the Bf 109's cockpit instrumentation, with a combined artificial horizon/turn and slip indicator replacing what had previously been just a turn and slip indicator.

Just four G-0 pre-production machines were built, though 40 had been planned, and none of them saw active service. The remaining 36 airframes were constructed as full production model G-1s

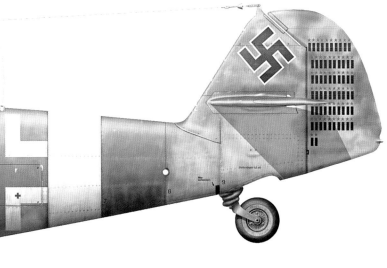

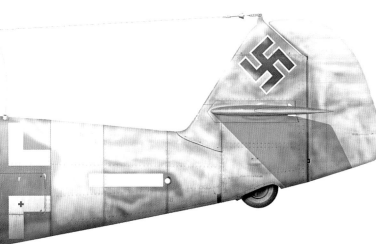

◀ ## BF 109 G-2

Unteroffizier Werner 'Quax' Quast flew White 9 with 4./JG 52 during early February 1943 while based at Slavyansk in the USSR. That month he destroyed 10 Soviet aircraft including a pair of Polikarpov I-153 biplanes.

LUFTWAFFE FIGHTERS — MESSERSCHMITT BF 109

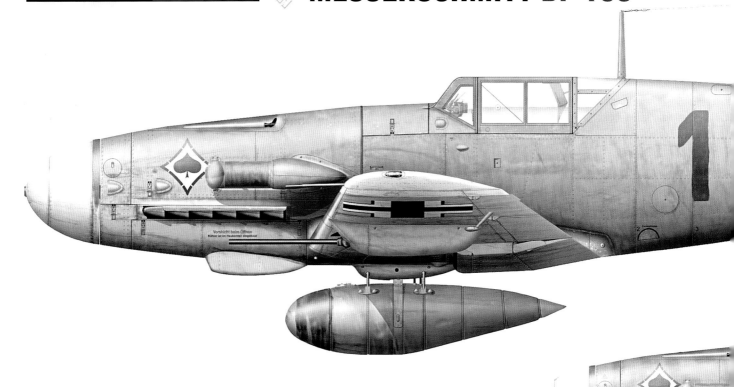

instead. Unusually, the Bf 109 G-1 and G-2 entered service at the same time in June 1942.

In fact, the G-2 was the standard fighter version with an unpressurised cockpit while the G-1 was a high-altitude type. The latter had a small, horn-shaped air intake for the cockpit compressor just above the supercharger intake, on the left of the upper cowling. The usual angled armour plate behind the pilot's head was replaced with a vertical plate that sealed off the cockpit from the rest of the fuselage. Each pane of the double glazed canopy had a small silica gel capsule inserted to soak up any moisture that might have become trapped inside.

In contrast, the G-2 had only single glazing and the F-4's standard angled head armour. G-2s were often fitted with drop tanks and underwing gondolas for 20mm MG 151/20 cannon.

While 1586 G-2s were built, there were only 167 G-1s.

The G-3 and G-4 mirrored the G-1 and G-2, with the G-4 being the standard unpressurised fighter. The G-4 appeared first, in November 1942, and was initially exactly the same as the G-2 except that it had the powerful new FuG 16 VHF radio set. This

had three times the range of its predecessor and offered a huge improvement in signal clarity. The antenna for this was moved to a position between frames seven and eight on the fuselage spine.

Later G-4s differed a little more in having larger mainwheels – 660 x 160mm compared to the previously fitted 650 x 150mm ones. There were also alterations to the undercarriage legs so that the wheels were more vertical, rather than sitting in parallel to the oleo legs. In order to accommodate this change, teardrop-shaped fairings were added to the upper wing surfaces above the wheel wells. The tailwheel was also enlarged to 350 x 135mm from 290 x 110mm.

A number of factory modifications were available for the G-4, including the G-4/R2 reconnaissance version, the G-4/R3 long-range reconnaissance version featuring a pair of 300 litre underwing droptanks, the G-4 Trop with filters for operating in harsh environments, the G-4/U3 reconnaissance version and the G-4Y command fighter.

Production of the pressurised G-3 began in January 1943 but only lasted a month, whereas G-4s continued to roll off production

BF 109 G-4 ▶

Having just completed his flight training in the autumn of 1942, Feldwebel Heinz Sachsenberg's first posting was to 6./JG 52, based in the southern sector of the Eastern Front. Between April and June 1943, he destroyed 15 Soviet aircraft. By June the unit was based at Anapa, USSR, and Sachsenberg's aircraft was Yellow 8.

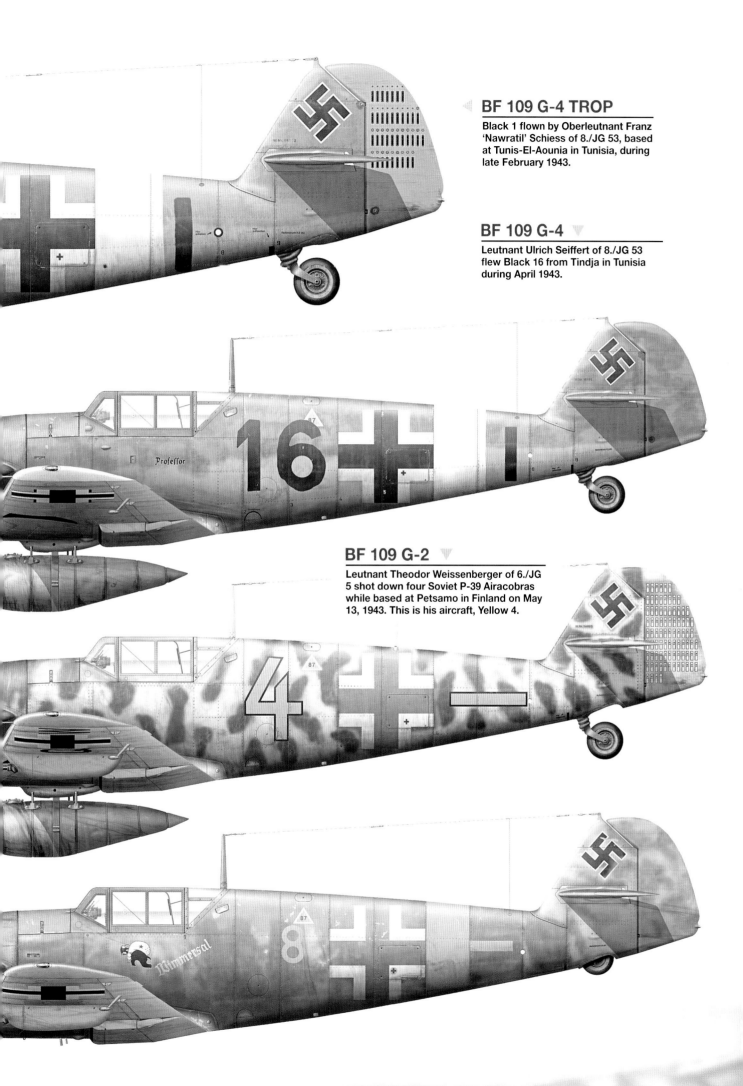

BF 109 G-4 TROP

Black 1 flown by Oberleutnant Franz 'Nawratil' Schiess of 8./JG 53, based at Tunis-El-Aounia in Tunisia, during late February 1943.

BF 109 G-4

Leutnant Ulrich Seiffert of 8./JG 53 flew Black 16 from Tindja in Tunisia during April 1943.

BF 109 G-2

Leutnant Theodor Weissenberger of 6./JG 5 shot down four Soviet P-39 Airacobras while based at Petsamo in Finland on May 13, 1943. This is his aircraft, Yellow 4.

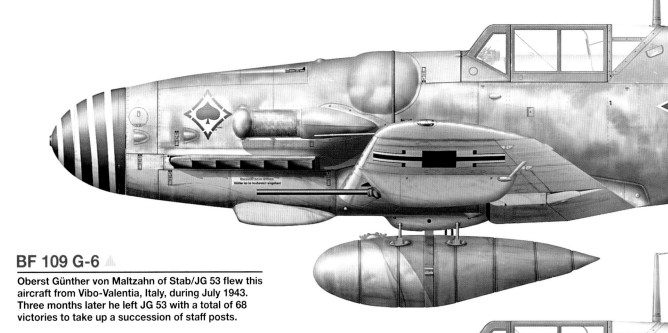

BF 109 G-6

Oberst Günther von Maltzahn of Stab/JG 53 flew this aircraft from Vibo-Valentia, Italy, during July 1943. Three months later he left JG 53 with a total of 68 victories to take up a succession of staff posts.

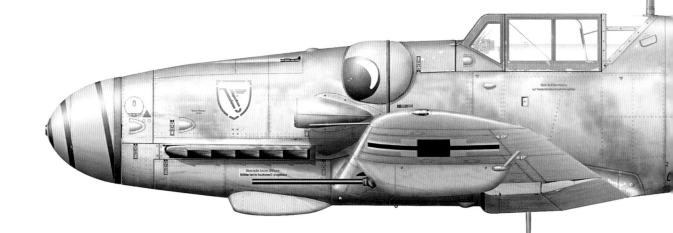

lines until July 1943. Just 50 G-3s were built compared to 1242 G-4s.

The same one-pressurised, one-unpressurised pattern was repeated with the G-5 and G-6. Once again, the unpressurised standard fighter appeared first – in February 1943. The Bf 109 G-6 finally saw the engine cowling-mounted 7.92mm MG 17s deleted

and in their place was fitted a pair of 13mm MG 131 machine guns. These larger guns required more room so a pair of large blisters appeared on the cowling over their breeches. In fact, this new bodywork was so substantial tests revealed that it reduced the aircraft's top speed by 6mph.

The G-5 did not appear until

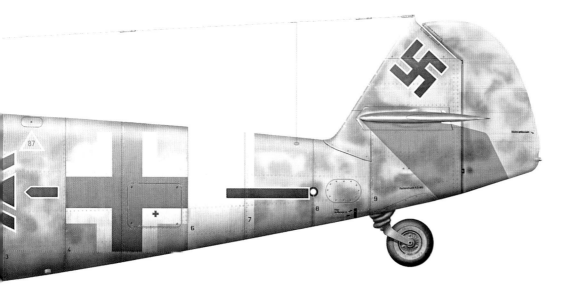

BF 109 G-2

Yellow 2 flown by Uffizier Kurt 'Poldi' Leopold of 3./JG 4, based in Mamaia, Romania, during August 1943.

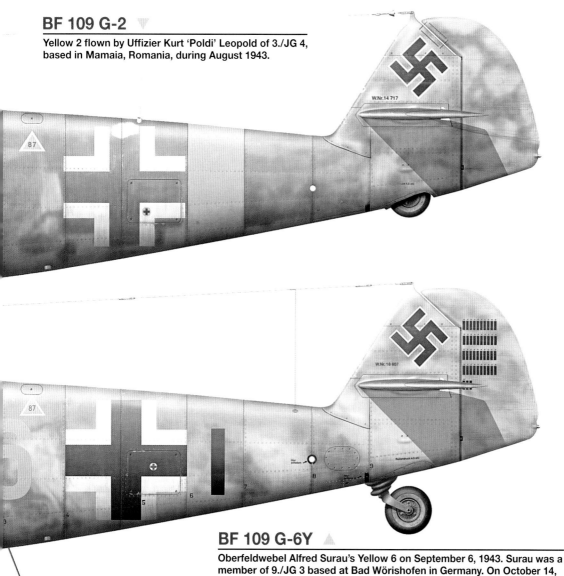

BF 109 G-6Y

Oberfeldwebel Alfred Surau's Yellow 6 on September 6, 1943. Surau was a member of 9./JG 3 based at Bad Wörishofen in Germany. On October 14, he shot down a B-17 for its 46th victory but was hit and badly wounded by return fire. He bailed out but died in hospital that same day.

May 1943 and except for its pressurised cockpit was largely identical to the G-6. Although it came nowhere near the vast production totals of its sibling, the G-5 was still produced in appreciable numbers, with 475 being built up to August 1944. At the time of the G-5's introduction, an enlarged wooden tail unit was added to the design – and that of later G-6s. Fitment of this new alteration was not standardised across all production lines, however, and numerous G-5s and later G-6s were built without it.

The new tail improved ground handing and served to reduce production costs but weighed more than the usual metal tail unit. This meant that a counterweight had to be fitted to the nose and the aircraft's overall weight was increased.

Production of the G-6 had ceased in June of 1944 after more than 16 months. The precise number made is impossible to discern since surviving factory records are

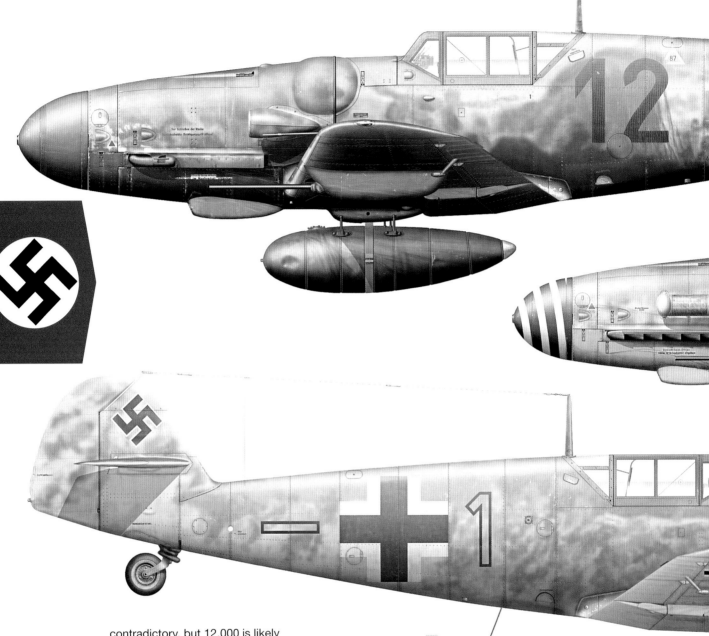

contradictory, but 12,000 is likely to be a conservative estimate.

While G-6 production was ongoing, several other improvements were steadily introduced into production lines. A new armoured glass head rest was developed which started to replace the original armour plate and towards the end of 1943 the new Erla Haube canopy was introduced. This featured a completely redesigned structure with larger areas of Perspex giving the pilot substantially improved visibility. In addition, where only the central portion of the old welded canopy opened on a hinge, the whole of the Erla Haube aft of the windscreen could be swung open to starboard. The new canopy was steadily added to new-build Bf 109 lines and retrofitted to some existing aircraft. Eventually it replaced the original canopy altogether.

BF 109 G-6

Hermann Graf, now a major, became the leader of JG 50 in August 1943 but the unit was disbanded in October 1943 and absorbed into I./JG 301. This is his Green 1 of Stab./JG 50 during September 1943 – a month when he shot down two B-17s and a de Havilland Mosquito.

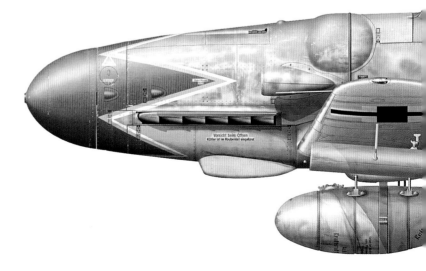

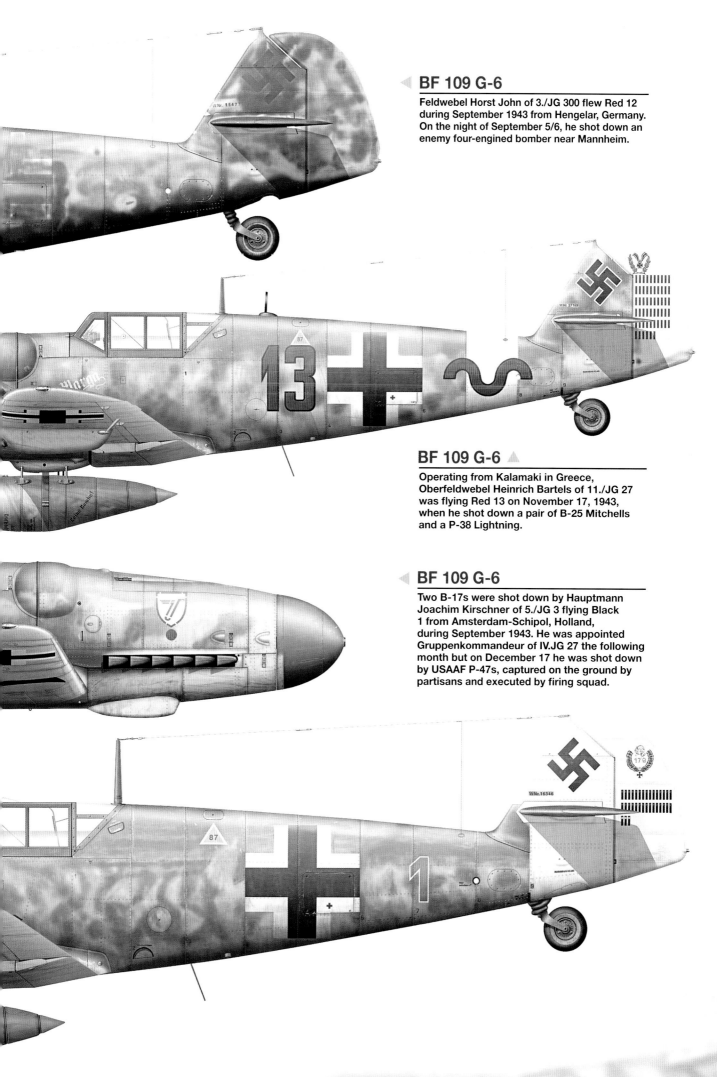

BF 109 G-6

Feldwebel Horst John of 3./JG 300 flew Red 12 during September 1943 from Hengelar, Germany. On the night of September 5/6, he shot down an enemy four-engined bomber near Mannheim.

BF 109 G-6

Operating from Kalamaki in Greece, Oberfeldwebel Heinrich Bartels of 11./JG 27 was flying Red 13 on November 17, 1943, when he shot down a pair of B-25 Mitchells and a P-38 Lightning.

BF 109 G-6

Two B-17s were shot down by Hauptmann Joachim Kirschner of 5./JG 3 flying Black 1 from Amsterdam-Schipol, Holland, during September 1943. He was appointed Gruppenkommandeur of IV.JG 27 the following month but on December 17 he was shot down by USAAF P-47s, captured on the ground by partisans and executed by firing squad.

MESSERSCHMITT BF 109

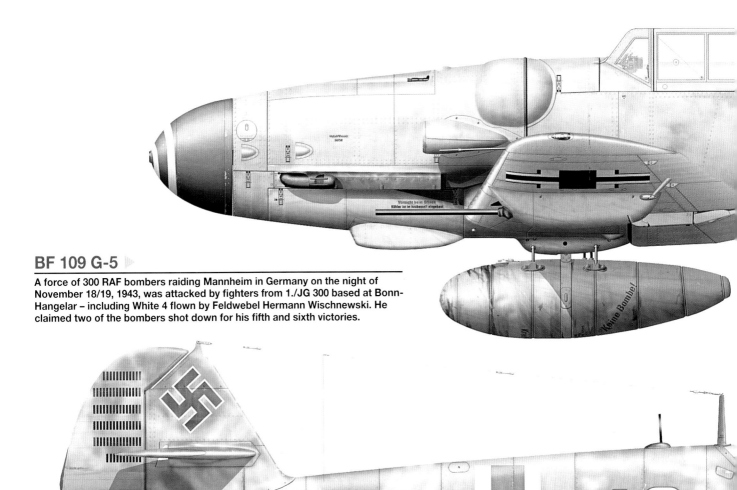

BF 109 G-5

A force of 300 RAF bombers raiding Mannheim in Germany on the night of November 18/19, 1943, was attacked by fighters from 1./JG 300 based at Bonn-Hangelar – including White 4 flown by Feldwebel Hermann Wischnewski. He claimed two of the bombers shot down for his fifth and sixth victories.

BF 109 G-6

Oberleutnant Robert Weiss of 10./JG 54, based at Libau in Latvia, was flying White 10 on January 17, 1944, when he shot down a trio of Il-2 bombers. The first went down at 10.50am, and the third at 10.56am.

BF 109 G-6

Hauptmann Gerhard Barkhorn of Stab II./JG 52, based at Bagerovo in the USSR, destroyed a pair of Yak-1s and a Soviet P-39 Airacobra on January 23, 1944, flying this G-6.

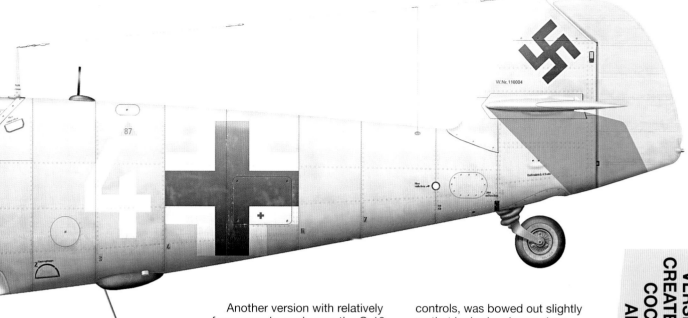

The G-8 was another version of the G-6, this time modified for reconnaissance work with only the engine cannon or the cowling guns fitted. In its fuselage, it carried either an Rb 12.5/7x5 or Rb 32/7x9 camera and an Rb 50/30. It saw only limited production.

Another version with relatively few example made was the G-12 – a two-seat trainer version of the Bf 109. These were created by adding a second cockpit to existing G-4 and G-6 airframes. This was done at the expense of fuel tank capacity and meant that 300 litre drop tanks had to be fitted as standard. Armament was reduced to just one or sometimes both cowling machine guns. The instructor's cockpit, which was at the rear and featured full flight controls, was bowed out slightly so that he had a clearer view.

A range of equipment upgrade kits was also available for the G-series. These included the R I under-fuselage bomb rack, R II under-fuselage bomb rack, R III fuselage droptank rack, R IV MK 108 underwing cannon gondolas and R VI MG 151/20 underwing gondolas.

In addition to these, the G-6 was also offered with a vast range of factory modifications to help it fulfil the widest possible range of functions. Among these were the G-6/R2 recce fighter with MW

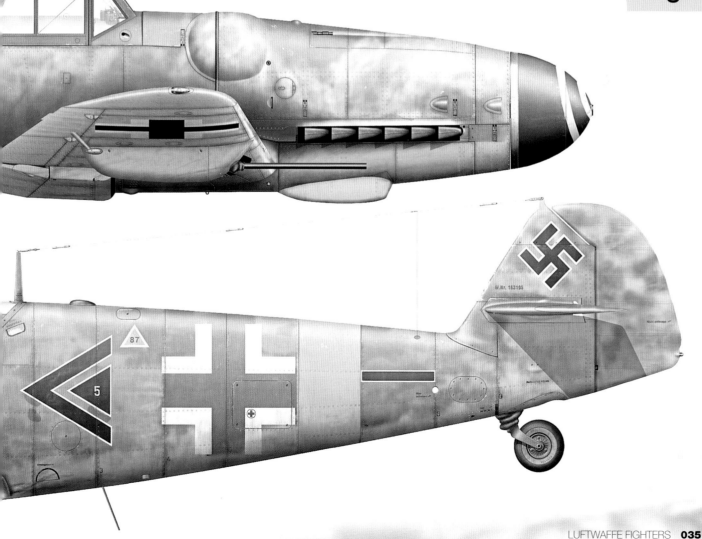

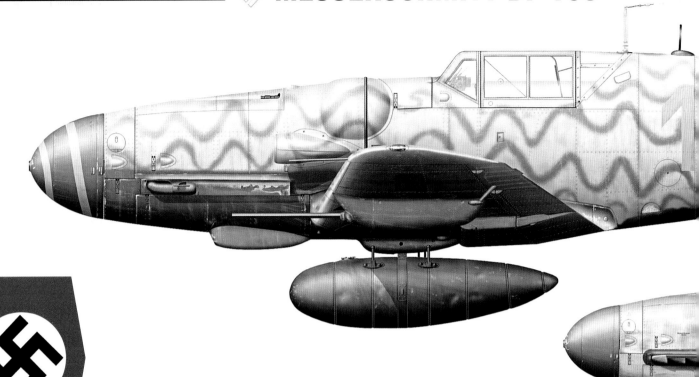

50 boost, the G-6/R3 long-range recce fighter with droptanks, the G-6/R4 with underwing cannon gondolas, the G-6 Trop, the G-6/U2 with GM-1 boost, the G-6/U3 recce fighter, the G-6/U4 with MK 108 engine cannon, G-6Y command fighter, G-6N night fighter which incorporated the R4 gondolas, and the G-6/U4 N which was the same as the G-6N but also featuring the MK 108 engine cannon.

The major Bf 109 G-6 production lines switched to building the G-14 in June-July 1944, with the earliest examples reaching front line units in France before the end of July. The G-14 was an attempt to standardise the Bf 109 again after the enormous variety of modifications that had

been added to the G-6 piecemeal in different factories so as not to interrupt production. It offered MW 50 water injection, which boosted power output to 1775hp, and the Erla Haube canopy was fitted as standard. A high altitude version, the G-14/AS, was also brought into production. This was equipped with the DB 605 ASM engine which had a larger capacity supercharger and was able to offer significantly improved performance above 24,000ft. Conservative estimates place the combined total number of G-14s and G-14/ASs built at 5500.

Throughout the production life of the G-6 and its offspring, Messerschmitt had been working on the next evolutionary step in the Bf 109's development – the

BF 109 G-6

Leutnant Paul Müngersdorff of 5./JG 2, based at Creil, France, was flying White 28 on March 18, 1944, at 3.20pm when he shot down a B-17 in the Strasbourg area.

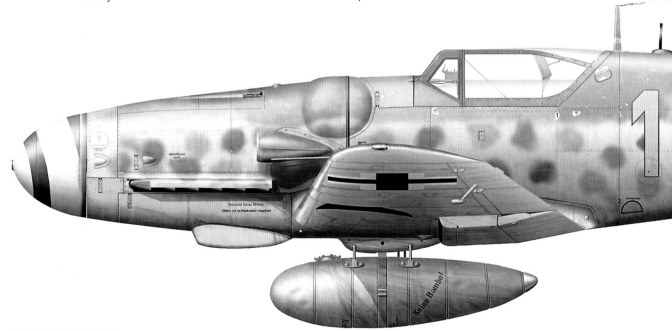

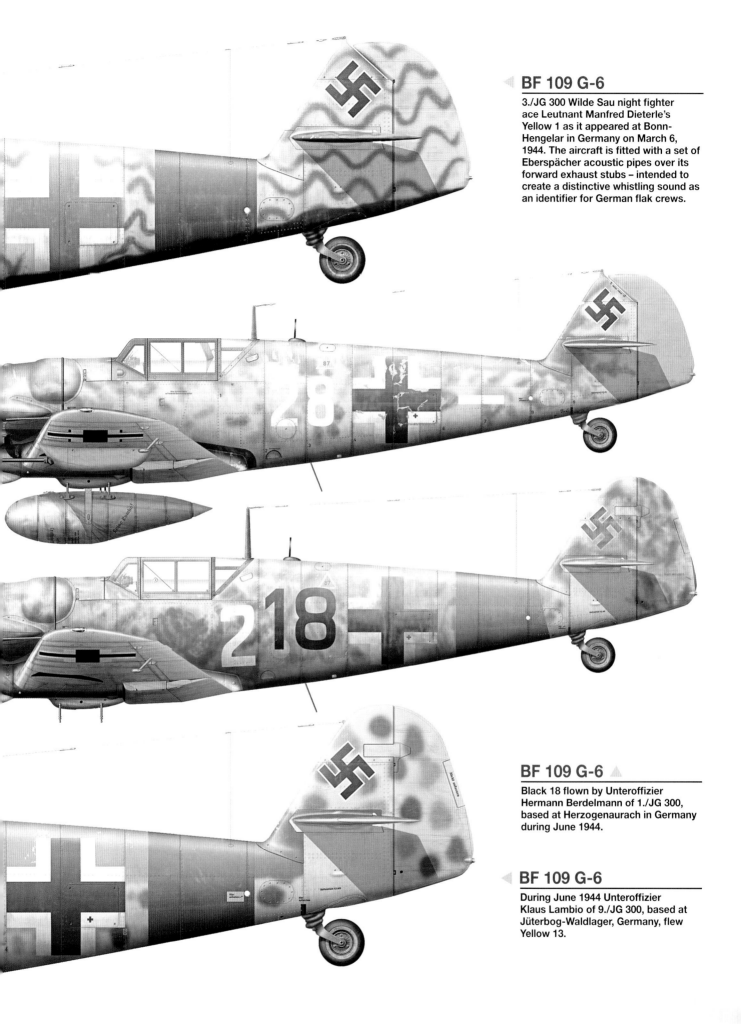

BF 109 G-6

3./JG 300 Wilde Sau night fighter ace Leutnant Manfred Dieterle's Yellow 1 as it appeared at Bonn-Hengelar in Germany on March 6, 1944. The aircraft is fitted with a set of Eberspächer acoustic pipes over its forward exhaust stubs – intended to create a distinctive whistling sound as an identifier for German flak crews.

BF 109 G-6

Black 18 flown by Unteroffizier Hermann Berdelmann of 1./JG 300, based at Herzogenaurach in Germany during June 1944.

BF 109 G-6

During June 1944 Unteroffizier Klaus Lambio of 9./JG 300, based at Jüterbog-Waldlager, Germany, flew Yellow 13.

MESSERSCHMITT BF 109

K series. It was meant to be fitted with the new DB 605 D engine but delays at Daimler-Benz meant that the Bf 109 K did not enter production until August 1944. By now the manufacturing of Bf 109s was a nationwide industry in Germany and it took time to gear up for the K. So in the meantime, with the engines now available and starting in October, established G-14 production lines at Erla, WNF and Messerschmitt's own factory at Regensburg began building DB 605 D-2-powered G-14s as the G-10.

The first G-10s began to enter service in November 1944, some of them apparently with both their original G-14 data plates and new G-10 plates following the fitment of the DB 605 D-2. G-10s were also fitted with the MW-50 boost as standard and had a slightly larger oil cooler fitted than that of the standard G-14s. Some 2600 G-10s are thought to have been made – with production continuing until the end of the war.

BF 109 K

The final version of the Bf 109, the K was the fighter's ultimate development. As early as March 1943, Reichsmarschall Hermann Göring had said: "The Me 109 is still an aircraft of very high performance. However, it has now reached the peak of its performance; no further improvement is possible: the aircraft cannot take a more powerful engine, whereas the British began to improve the Spitfire series very early with the result that this aircraft is now

BF 109 G-14/AS

Tussling with USAAF P-47s on October 6, 1944, the G-14 of Leutnant Walter Köhne, Yellow 1, suffered critical damage, forcing him to make a belly landing at Bretscheid. He was able to return to his unit, 6./JG 11, based at Wunsdorf in Germany, unscathed.

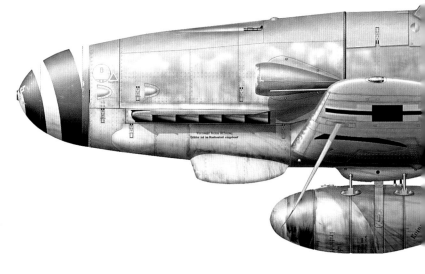

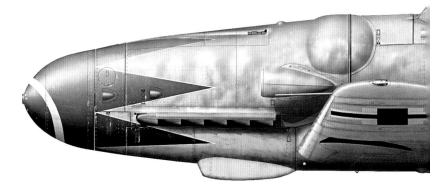

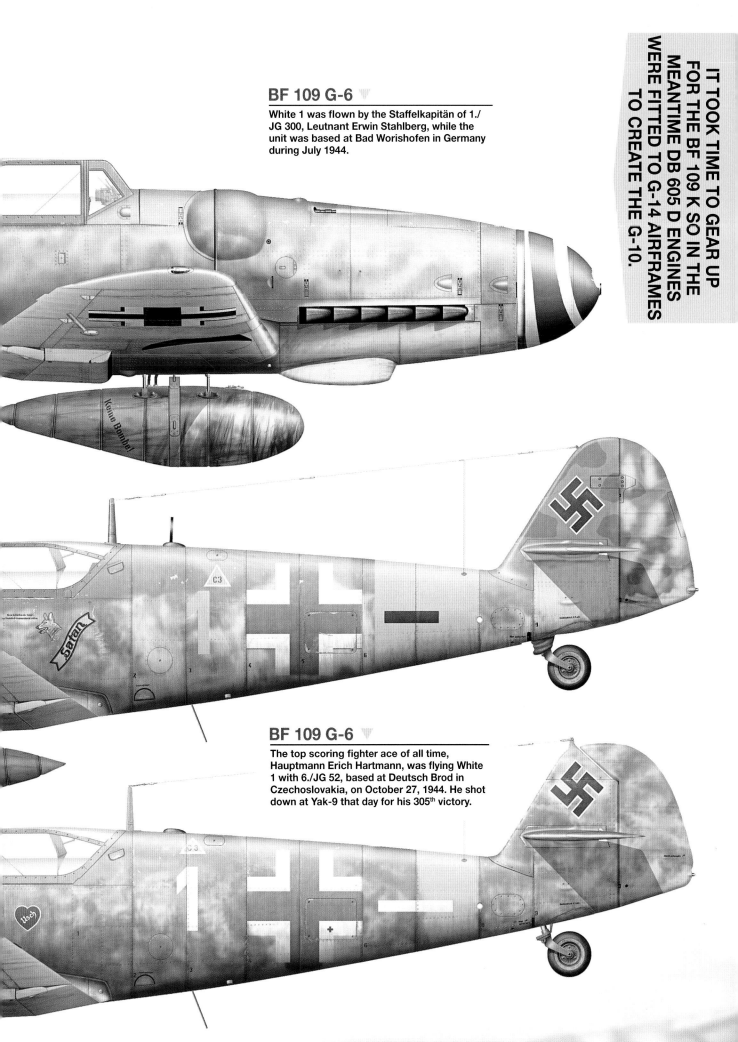

IT TOOK TIME TO GEAR UP FOR THE BF 109 K SO IN THE MEANTIME DB 605 D ENGINES WERE FITTED TO G-14 AIRFRAMES TO CREATE THE G-10.

BF 109 G-6

White 1 was flown by the Staffelkapitän of 1./JG 300, Leutnant Erwin Stahlberg, while the unit was based at Bad Worishofen in Germany during July 1944.

BF 109 G-6

The top scoring fighter ace of all time, Hauptmann Erich Hartmann, was flying White 1 with 6./JG 52, based at Deutsch Brod in Czechoslovakia, on October 27, 1944. He shot down at Yak-9 that day for his 305th victory.

MESSERSCHMITT BF 109

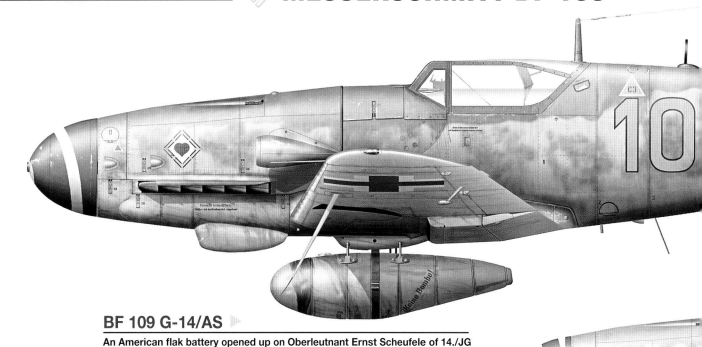

BF 109 G-14/AS

An American flak battery opened up on Oberleutnant Ernst Scheufele of 14./JG 4 while he was flying Black 2 over Saxony on December 3, 1944. His aircraft was wrecked and he was wounded. Having bailed out, he was taken prisoner on the ground. At the time, his unit was based at Frankfurt-Main in Germany.

absolutely and unquestionably superior to the Me 109."

Messerschmitt had proven him wrong time and again. And now, with the Bf 109 K, the company succeeded in producing one of the best piston-engined aircraft of the war. It was intended to iron out old flaws in the type's design and provide full interchangeability of parts, as well as being easier to build and using up fewer strategically important materials than any

previous model through the extensive use of plywood parts.

The only version to see quantity production was the K-4. This could be distinguished from earlier models by a relocation of the radio equipment hatch to a position higher up between frames four and five, and a repositioning of the fuselage fuel tank filler point to between frames two and three. The D/F loop moved rearwards to a point between frames three and four on the fuselage spine. The Bf 109 K-4 rudder had a Flettner tab as standard and a long fully retractable tailwheel was added;

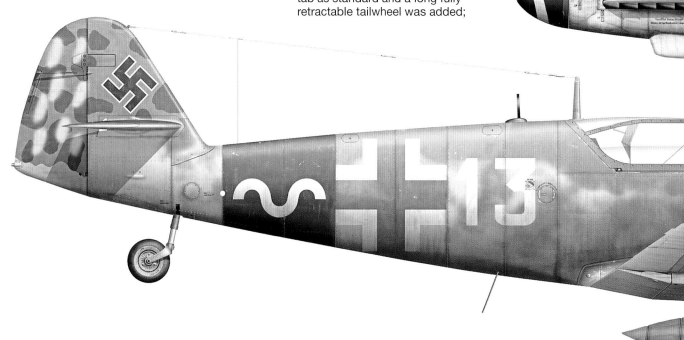

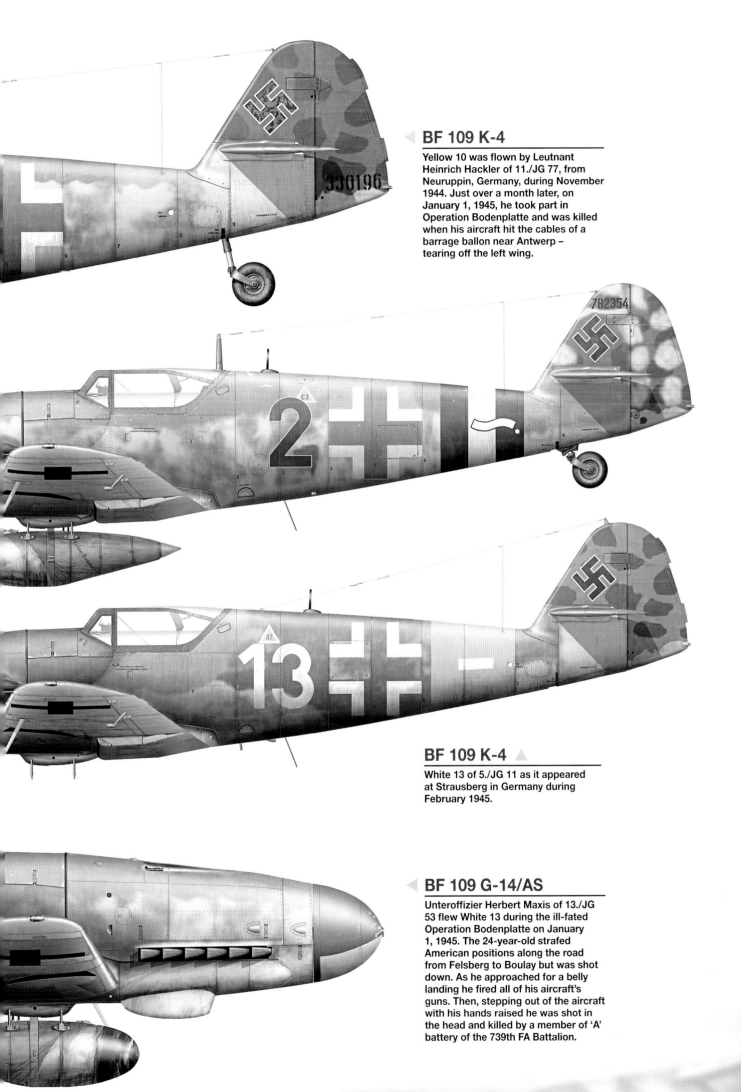

BF 109 K-4

Yellow 10 was flown by Leutnant Heinrich Hackler of 11./JG 77, from Neuruppin, Germany, during November 1944. Just over a month later, on January 1, 1945, he took part in Operation Bodenplatte and was killed when his aircraft hit the cables of a barrage ballon near Antwerp – tearing off the left wing.

BF 109 K-4

White 13 of 5./JG 11 as it appeared at Strausberg in Germany during February 1945.

BF 109 G-14/AS

Unteroffizier Herbert Maxis of 13./JG 53 flew White 13 during the ill-fated Operation Bodenplatte on January 1, 1945. The 24-year-old strafed American positions along the road from Felsberg to Boulay but was shot down. As he approached for a belly landing he fired all of his aircraft's guns. Then, stepping out of the aircraft with his hands raised he was shot in the head and killed by a member of 'A' battery of the 739th FA Battalion.

MESSERSCHMITT BF 109

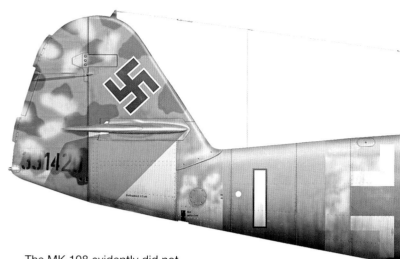

THE MK 108 CANNON EVIDENTLY DID NOT REACT WELL TO VIOLENT MANOEUVRING DURING COMBAT AND FREQUENTLY JAMMED – LEAVING THE PILOT WITH JUST THE COWLING MACHINE GUNS.

the wheel itself measuring 350 x 135mm. Two small doors closed over the tailwheel recess to provide a smooth aerodynamic form.

There were large rectangular fairings for the type's big 660 x 190mm main undercarriage wheels and doors covered the wheels when they were retracted – though these were often removed by front line units. The K-4 was fitted with a FuG 16ZY radio set, the aerial extending from the underside of the port outer wing, a FuG 25a IFF and FuG 125 Hermine D/F equipment.

Standard armament was an engine-mounted MK 108 or MG 151/20 and a pair of MG 131s in the nose with 300 rounds per gun. Underwing gondolas fitted with additional MG 151/20s were an occasional upgrade and other alternative Rüstsätze included 300 litre drop tanks, bombs up to 500kg and Wfr.Gr. 21 rockets.

The MK 108 evidently did not react well to violent manoeuvring during combat and frequently jammed – leaving the pilot with just the cowling machine guns. The Bf 109 K-4's gunsight was the standard Revi 16C. There had been plans to replace it with the EZ 42 Gyro gunsight but none of these were ever installed.

Early K-4s were powered by the DB 605 DM but this was quickly replaced with the DB 605 DB/DC. This versatile unit included an adjustment screw which allowed mechanics to set it for either B4 fuel with MW 50 Methanol Water injection or C3 fuel with or without MW 50 boost. Running on C3 fuel with MW 50, the DB 605 DC could supply an astonishing 1971hp – with the fully loaded K-4 weighing

BF 109 K-4

Yellow 13 was flown by Feldwebel Bruno Nüser of 15./JG 53, based at Stuttgart-Echterdingen, Germany, on March 13, 1945.

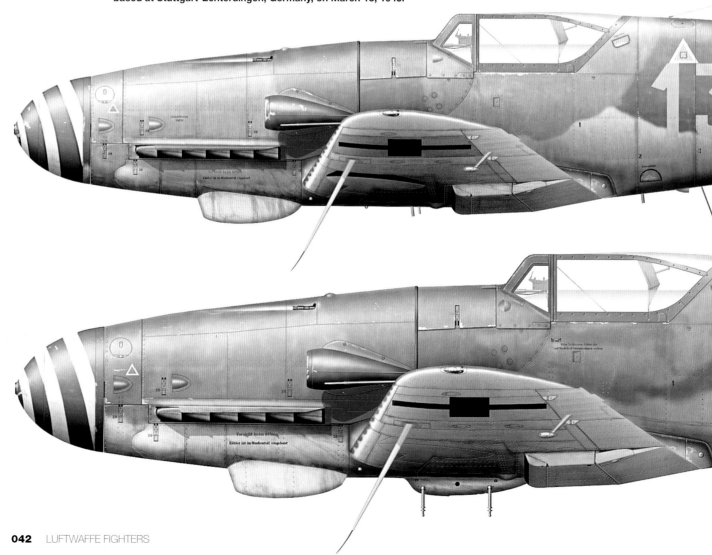

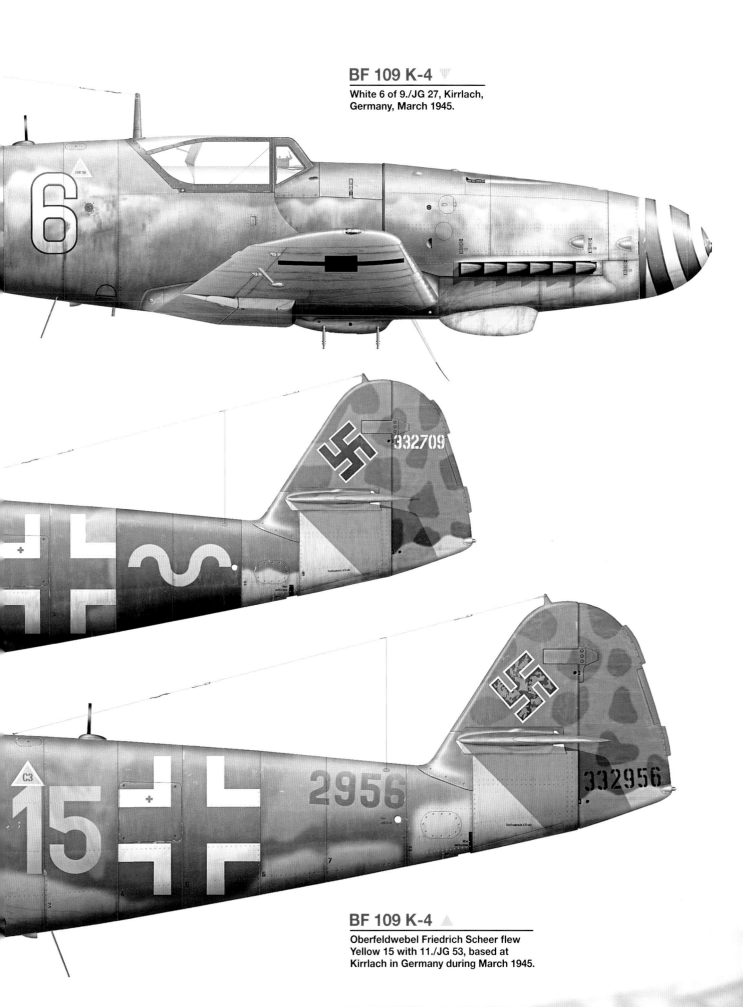

BF 109 K-4

White 6 of 9./JG 27, Kirrlach,
Germany, March 1945.

BF 109 K-4

Oberfeldwebel Friedrich Scheer flew
Yellow 15 with 11./JG 53, based at
Kirrlach in Germany during March 1945.

MESSERSCHMITT BF 109

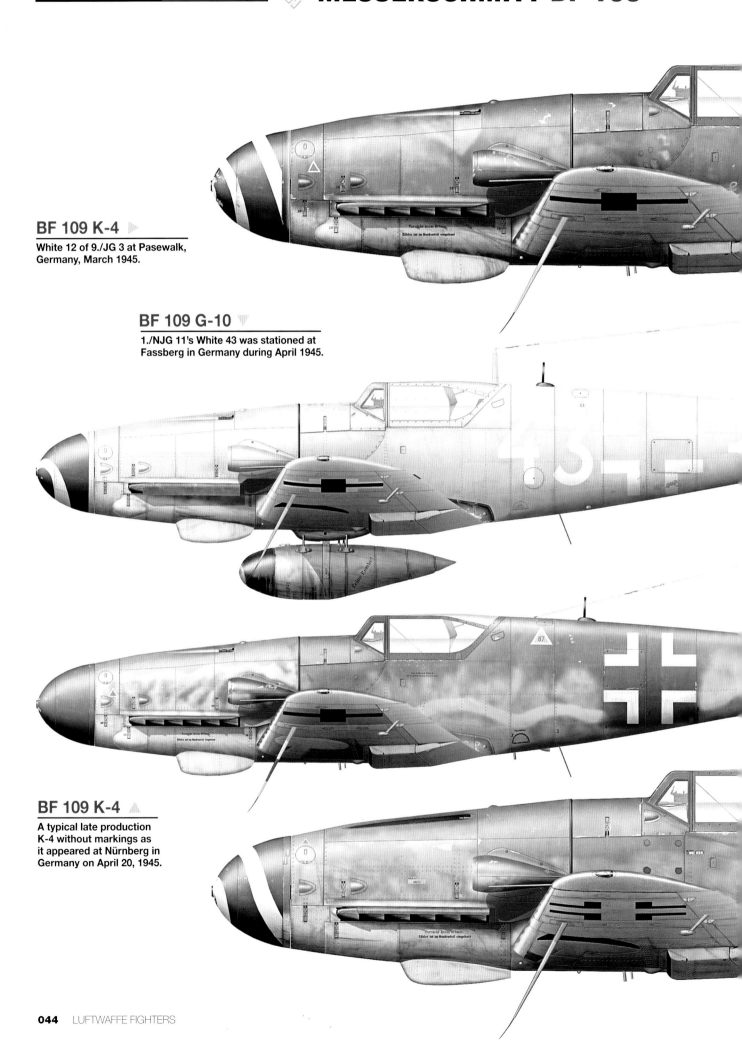

BF 109 K-4 ▶

White 12 of 9./JG 3 at Pasewalk, Germany, March 1945.

BF 109 G-10 ▽

1./NJG 11's White 43 was stationed at Fassberg in Germany during April 1945.

BF 109 K-4 ▲

A typical late production K-4 without markings as it appeared at Nürnberg in Germany on April 20, 1945.

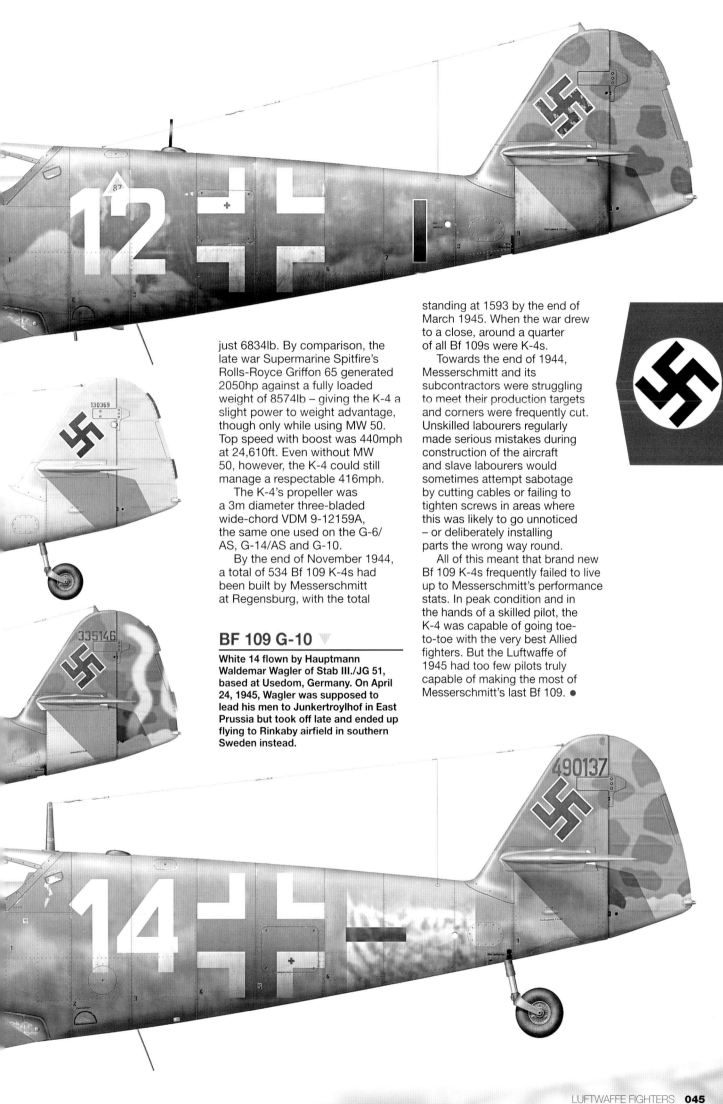

just 6834lb. By comparison, the late war Supermarine Spitfire's Rolls-Royce Griffon 65 generated 2050hp against a fully loaded weight of 8574lb – giving the K-4 a slight power to weight advantage, though only while using MW 50. Top speed with boost was 440mph at 24,610ft. Even without MW 50, however, the K-4 could still manage a respectable 416mph.

The K-4's propeller was a 3m diameter three-bladed wide-chord VDM 9-12159A, the same one used on the G-6/AS, G-14/AS and G-10.

By the end of November 1944, a total of 534 Bf 109 K-4s had been built by Messerschmitt at Regensburg, with the total

BF 109 G-10 ▽

White 14 flown by Hauptmann Waldemar Wagler of Stab III./JG 51, based at Usedom, Germany. On April 24, 1945, Wagler was supposed to lead his men to Junkertroylhof in East Prussia but took off late and ended up flying to Rinkaby airfield in southern Sweden instead.

standing at 1593 by the end of March 1945. When the war drew to a close, around a quarter of all Bf 109s were K-4s.

Towards the end of 1944, Messerschmitt and its subcontractors were struggling to meet their production targets and corners were frequently cut. Unskilled labourers regularly made serious mistakes during construction of the aircraft and slave labourers would sometimes attempt sabotage by cutting cables or failing to tighten screws in areas where this was likely to go unnoticed – or deliberately installing parts the wrong way round.

All of this meant that brand new Bf 109 K-4s frequently failed to live up to Messerschmitt's performance stats. In peak condition and in the hands of a skilled pilot, the K-4 was capable of going toe-to-toe with the very best Allied fighters. But the Luftwaffe of 1945 had too few pilots truly capable of making the most of Messerschmitt's last Bf 109. ●

MESSERSCHMITT BF 109

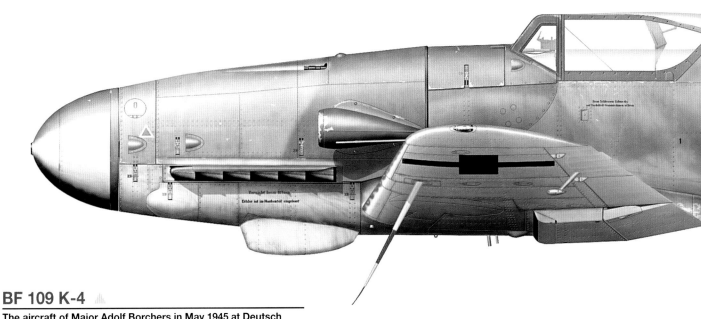

BF 109 K-4

The aircraft of Major Adolf Borchers in May 1945 at Deutsch Brod in Czechoslovakia. Borchers became the commander of III./JG 52 on February 1, 1945, and surrendered to US forces when the war ended – only to be handed over to the Soviets. His final total of victories was 132.

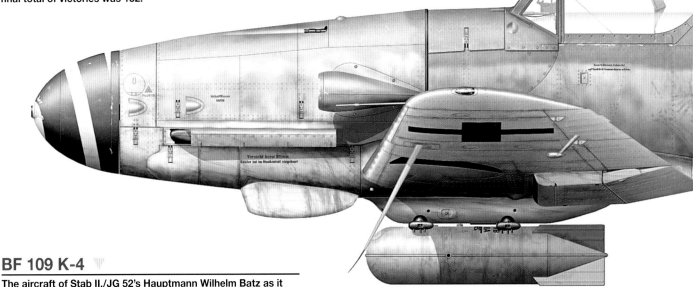

BF 109 K-4

The aircraft of Stab II./JG 52's Hauptmann Wilhelm Batz as it appeared at Zeltweg in Austria on May 5, 1945. At the end of the war, Batz and his Gruppe evaded Soviet captivity by escaping from Hungary, where they had been stationed, and returning to Germany via Austria. He scored a total of 237 victories.

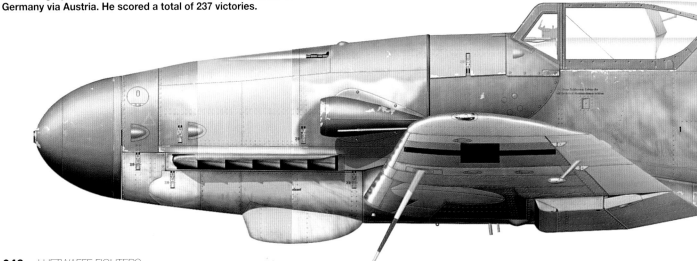

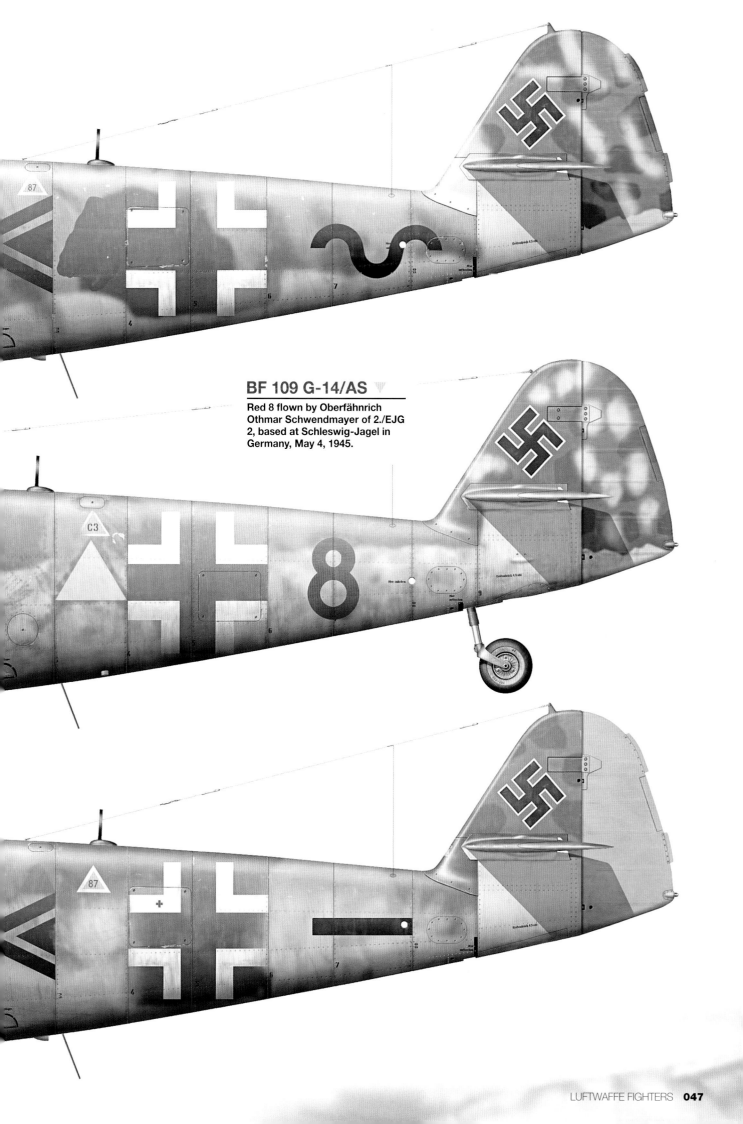

BF 109 G-14/AS

Red 8 flown by Oberfähnrich Othmar Schwendmayer of 2./EJG 2, based at Schleswig-Jagel in Germany, May 4, 1945.

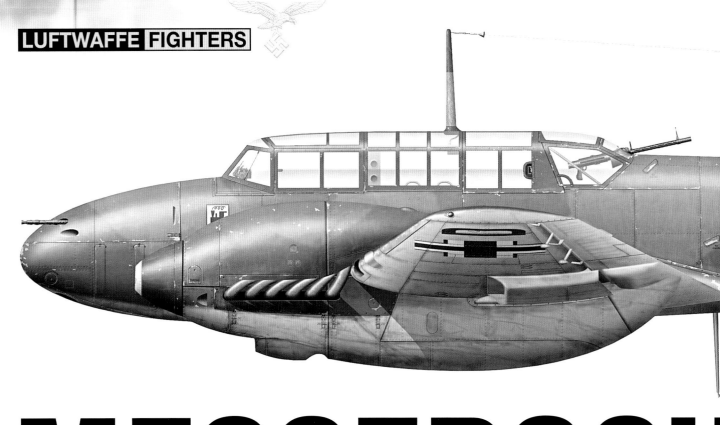

MESSERSCH

1935-1945

Doomed to forever play second fiddle to Messerschmitt's world-beating Bf 109, the twin-engined Bf 110 nevertheless became a success in its own right. The type's early promise evaporated when it suffered heavy losses during the Battle of Britain but later in the war, when it was deployed as a radar-equipped night fighter against the RAF's heavy bomber fleet, it became a fearsome hunter – picking off Allied aircraft as they traversed occupied Europe to and from their targets.

Bf 110 D-0

The enormous Dackelbauch ventral fuel tank intended to significantly extend the Bf 110's range is evident on M8+FH of 6./ZG 76. This is how it appeared at Stavanger-Forus in Norway during June 1940.

W hen plans for Germany's new air force were being laid during the early 1930s, it was decided that among the categories of aircraft required would be a Kampfzerstörer – a twin-engine two-seater heavy fighter with the ability to carry bombs or other equipment to fulfil a wide range of roles.

A requirement for this multirole machine was issued in 1934 to Arado, Focke-Wulf, Gotha, Henschel and Messerschmitt. The Arado and Gotha designs were evidently dismissed at an early stage but the other three manufacturers were presented

with orders for prototype aircraft. Focke-Wulf produced the physically massive and enormously heavy Fw 57, Henschel built the Hs 124 which was similar to the Fw 57 in layout if not size, and Messerschmitt constructed the Bf 110.

During mid-1935, however, it was decided that an aircraft expected to do so many jobs would be too much of a compromise and a new requirement was issued which effectively divided the Kampfzerstörer concept into two: a Schnellbomber or 'fast bomber' and a Zerstörer or 'destroyer', a heavy fighter. The Focke-Wulf and Henschel designs were

Bf 110 C-1

A Gloster Gladiator flown by Sergeant Per Schye of the Norwegian Fighter Wing was shot down over Bratenjordet on April 9, 1940, by Leutnant Helmut Lent. Lent, of I./ZG 76, based at Fornebu in Norway was flying M8+DH.

MITT BF 110

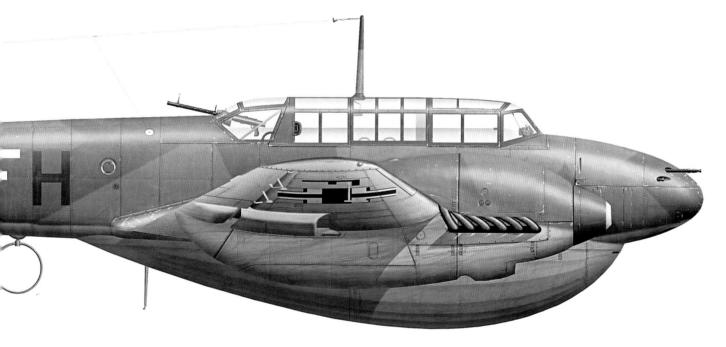

deemed incapable of meeting either requirement and were dismissed, leaving only the Bf 110 in the running for the Zerstörer contract. Another version of the Bf 110, the Bf 162, was designed to compete as a Schnellbomber against two new designs – the Junkers Ju 88 and the Henschel Hs 127.

The Bf 110 V1 first flew on May 12, 1936, with the civilian registration D-AHOA. It was a low-wing monoplane with twin rudders, Handley Page leading edge slats and a retractable tailwheel, powered by a pair of Daimler-Benz DB 600 A engines. Further test flights followed and the Bf 110 V2 took to

the air for the first time on October 24, 1936. The V3 was the first example to be fitted with weapons – a quartet of MG 17s in the nose.

The 986hp DB 600 was proving to be unreliable however, and for the first batch of Bf 110 A-0s a pair of 610hp Jumo 210 Bs was substituted. Just four A-0s were built, between August 1937 and March 1938, due to the engine's poor performance. Two examples of a revised variant, the Bf 110 B-0, were produced during early 1938. This featured a non-retractable tailwheel, slightly lengthened fuselage and reshaped nose, and

MESSERSCHMITT BF 110

Bf 110 C

One of the most successful Zerstörer pilots who flew during the Battle of Britain was Oberleutnant Theodor Rossiwall of 6./ZG 26. He is credited with five victories during the battle and shot down 19 enemy aircraft during 400 missions overall. 3U+AP was his aircraft during July 1940 while based at St Omer-Crècy in France.

was intended to receive the DB 600 A now that Daimler-Benz had seemingly got to grips with its earlier difficulties. However, the two machines were initially flight tested with Jumo 210 Gs. Armament was upgraded to include a pair of MG FF 20mm cannon in addition to the MG 17s and a single MG 15 machine gun was installed in the rear cockpit.

With the DB 600 still unavailable, another eight B-0s were then built with 210 Gs. These were soon supplemented by 40 production model B-1s which all had the same powerplant – easily identifiable by the large radiator fitted beneath each engine. By the end of 1938 the DB 600 had been dropped and the DB 601 B-1 engine chosen to power the next Bf 110 variant – the C series. The DB 601s' radiators were fitted under the aircraft's wings, slightly outboard of each engine nacelle. Beneath the nacelles themselves were small oil coolers and air scoops. Rounded wingtips, which had been a feature of all previous Bf 110s, were replaced with squared off tips.

A series of 10 pre-production C-0s were built, followed by the full production C-1. The first of these were delivered to Luftwaffe units in early 1939 and a total of 195 were made up to the beginning of the Second World War. Further variants of the C series included the C-2, which had a FuG 10 radio fitted, the C-3 which had its MG FF cannon upgraded to MG FF/Ms, the C-4 which had better armour protection for the crew and the C-4/B which added a pair of bomb racks to the basic C-4. The line was further extended with the C-5 reconnaissance version, which had both MG FFs removed and an Rb 50/30 camera installed, the C-6 with a single MK 101 30mm cannon attached via an under-fuselage mount and a C-7 based on the C-4/B but with centreline bomb racks able to carry double the payload – two 500kg bombs compared to the earlier design's two 250kg bombs.

Work on the Bf 110 D long-range variant had begun during the second half of 1939. This was designed, initially, to extend the standard Bf 110 C's operational range by adding a large and ungainly-looking fuel tank to the aircraft's underside. This streamlined tank extended from halfway back under the nose to the rear of the crew canopy and could hold 1050 litres of additional fuel. Its bulbous appearance resulted in it receiving the nickname 'Dackelbauch' or dachshund's belly and the huge additional drag it created meant it was largely dropped after the initial run of Bf 110 D-0 pre-production machines, which had been converted from existing C series aircraft.

The D-1 was set up to accommodate a pair of 900 litre drop tanks, one under each wing, but was also designed with fittings for an improved Dackelbauch. Those that actually received the tank were designated D-1/R1, while those that had the drop tanks instead were the D-1/R2 – the 'R' standing for Rüstsätz.

Bf 110 C

The Staffelkapitän of 6./ZG 26, Oberleutnant Heinz Nacke, piloted M8+NP during August 1940. Based at Cherbourg-West in France, he destroyed two Hurricanes on August 15 and another three on August 30.

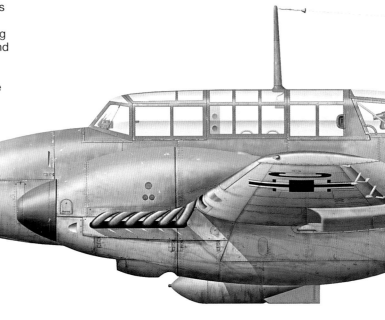

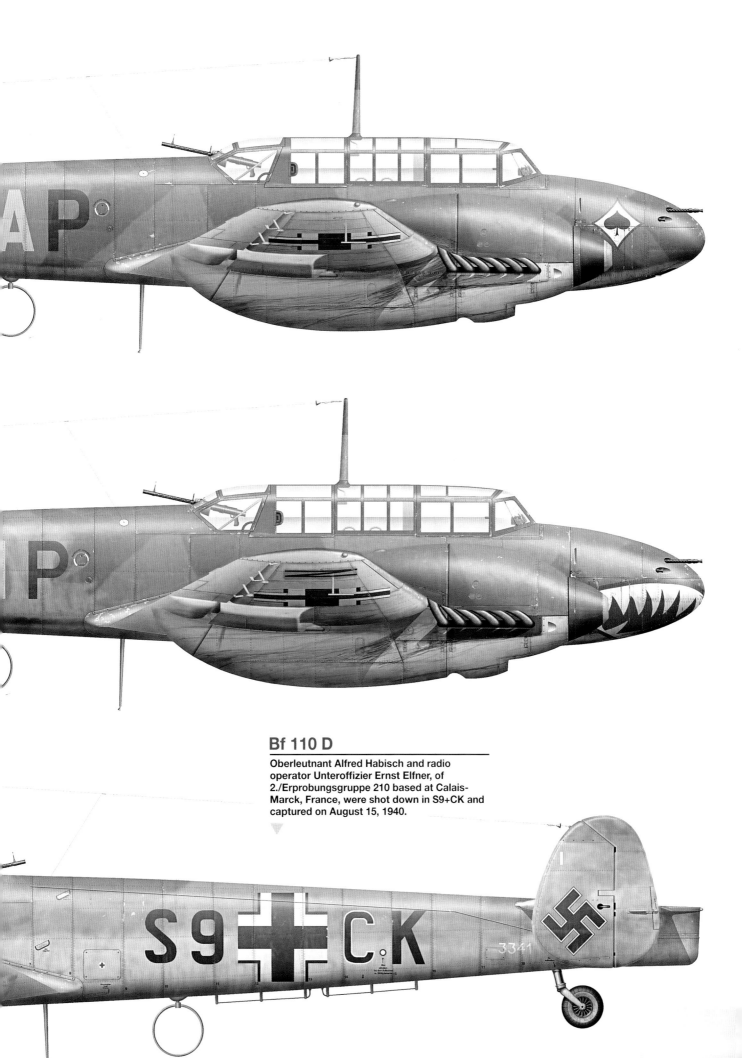

Bf 110 D

Oberleutnant Alfred Habisch and radio operator Unteroffizier Ernst Elfner, of 2./Erprobungsgruppe 210 based at Calais-Marck, France, were shot down in S9+CK and captured on August 15, 1940.

MESSERSCHMITT BF 110

Bf 110 C

Flying the aircraft of his unit's commanding officer Erich Groth, Oberleutnant Hermann Weeber of Stab II./ZG 76 made an emergency landing at Cousley Wood, East Sussex, on September 4, 1940. Groth's victory markings are recorded on the tail of M8+AC.

Bf 110 C

Bf 110s of V.(Z.)/LG 1, based at Ligescourt, France, were escorting Ju 88s on a bombing mission over England on September 27, 1940, when they were attacked by waves of Hurricanes and their formation was broken. L1+XB, flown by Hauptmann Horst Liensberger, was chased by Flying Officer Percy Burton of 249 Squadron until Burton rammed him – causing both aircraft to crash. Liensberger, his radio operator and Burton were all killed.

The D-2 kept the drop tanks but added centreline racks for a pair of 500kg bombs, while the D-3 featured a lengthened tail so that a rescue dingy could be installed. Either 300 litre or 900 litre drop tanks could be added with the two bomb racks as an optional replacement. The final 'D' variant was the D-4, which again retained the drop tanks but had both MG FFs removed and an Rb 50/30 camera fitted.

The Bf 110 had proven itself a capable enough fighter up to the beginning of the war but during the Battle of Britain it struggled to match the capabilities of the nimble Spitfire and Hurricanes fielded by the RAF. By the end of

1940 Messerschmitt was already lining up its replacement, the Me 210, which was expected to offer true multirole capability as well as far exceeding the abilities of the Bf 110 in all of its existing roles. However, the Me 210 was dogged by developmental problems that kept it from entering front line service in any great numbers. Messerschmitt therefore continued to work on the Bf 110 – which had by now also begun a new career as a night fighter.

Starting during the summer of 1940, night fighter units were equipped with a mixture of Bf 110 Cs and Ds and enjoyed some measure of success against increasingly obsolete RAF

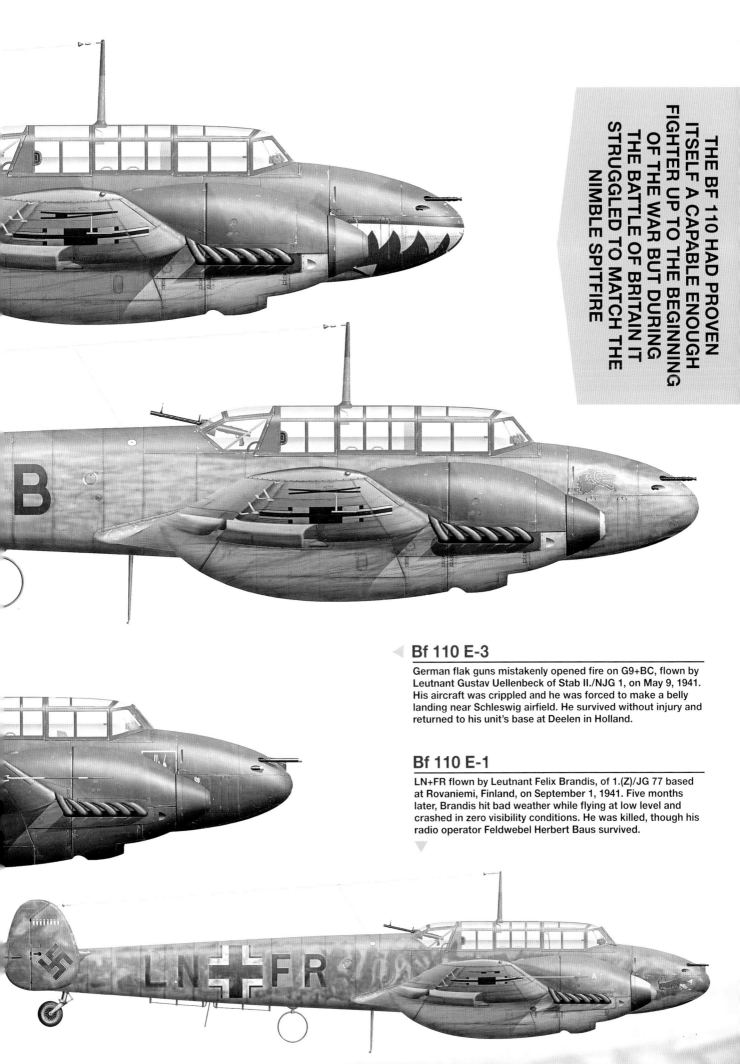

Bf 110 E-3

German flak guns mistakenly opened fire on G9+BC, flown by Leutnant Gustav Uellenbeck of Stab II./NJG 1, on May 9, 1941. His aircraft was crippled and he was forced to make a belly landing near Schleswig airfield. He survived without injury and returned to his unit's base at Deelen in Holland.

Bf 110 E-1

LN+FR flown by Leutnant Felix Brandis, of 1.(Z)/JG 77 based at Rovaniemi, Finland, on September 1, 1941. Five months later, Brandis hit bad weather while flying at low level and crashed in zero visibility conditions. He was killed, though his radio operator Feldwebel Herbert Baus survived.

MESSERSCHMITT BF 110

types such as the Handley Page Hampden, Vickers Wellington and Armstrong Whitworth Whitley. Initially, the night fighter Bf 110s were unmodified and sought out their prey with the aid of searchlights on the ground but they were quickly fitted with features such as exhaust flame dampers and improved radios.

The Bf 110 was particularly well suited to operations against the RAF's bomber fleet after dark because its large canopy offered much better visibility than that of a Bf 109, it could stay in the air longer to stalk the enemy, and it packed a powerful enough punch to quickly disable or destroy a large aircraft. At night, its relative lack of manoeuvrability was not a problem.

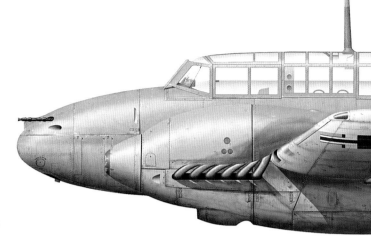

The next step in the Bf 110's development was the E, which was designed as a fighter-bomber, rather than a bomber escort or heavy fighter. It was fitted with four underwing racks able to carry a 50kg load each plus a fuselage centreline rack. It also offered further improved armour protection for the crew and the fuselage was strengthened to cope with the heavy munitions it was expected to carry. Pre-production E-0 examples were powered by DB 601 B engines but Messerschmitt switched to the newly available DB 601 P for the full production E-1. Armament was the same as that of the C-4. There were only two other variants though – the E-2, which had the same fuselage extension as the D-3 and the reconnaissance version E-3, which had the usual omission of MG FFs and Rb 50/30 camera installed.

The additional weight of armour and fuselage strengthening combined to make the Bf 110 E unwieldy and difficult to fly well. Production of it began in August 1940 and was still ongoing when the Bf 110 F was introduced in December 1941. A total of 856 Es

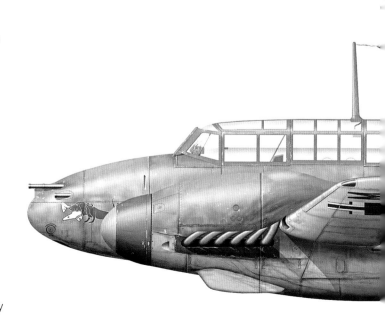

were built
all together, up to January
1942. The Bf 110 F retained the armour
and stronger fuselage of the E but had DB 601
F engines that were powerful enough to restore the type's performance to adequate levels. There were four versions of the Bf 110 F – the F-1 fighter-bomber, F-2 long range heavy fighter with the bomb racks deleted, F-3 recce version and the F-4 night fighter.

During 1941, the Bf 110 night fighters had been equipped with a new device intended to help them identify their targets in the dark – an infrared torch system known as the Spanner-Anlage which was mounted within the pilot's windscreen. This was deemed a failure however, as was its replacement the Spanner II which was meant to detect the heat from bomber engine exhausts.

The Bf 110 F-4 differed from the rest of the F series in two important respects: it was the first model to be fitted with the FuG 202 Lichtenstein radar set – which required aerials that protruded from the aircraft's nose like antlers – and it had a crew of three. Tests of Lichtenstein began in February 1942 and by the summer it was being used operationally. The F-4 was armed with four MG 17s, its rear-firing MG 15 and a pair of MG 151s replacing the usual MG FFs. Some aircraft had a pair of MK 108s fitted in a ventral pack too, providing truly devastating firepower. A pair of drop tanks was also fitted as standard.

Some 512 Bf 110 Fs were made before the series was finally switched entirely to its final iteration – the Bf 110 G.

Bf 110 D-1

2F+MA of Stab/StG. 3, based at Gambut in Libya, December 1941.

Bf 110 E-1

Oberleutnant Wilhelm 'Willy' Herget of 4./NJG 1 flew G9+HM from Herdla in Norway. This is how the aircraft appeared on February 20, 1942.

Bf 110 F-2

LV+MR flown by Oberfeldwebel Theodor Weissenberger of 6.(Z)/JG 5, based at Kirkenes in Norway, June 1942. A month earlier, on May 10, he shot down five enemy aircraft between 4.45pm and 4.57pm during a Ju 87 escort mission – becoming an 'ace in a day'.

MESSERSCHMITT BF 110

Bf 110 D-3

On the night of May 30/31, 1942, St Trond-based 4./NJG 1 intercepted RAF bombers heading for Cologne. Oberleutnant Walter Barte destroyed a Wellington at 1.46am and another 11 minutes later. He then went after a crippled Manchester being flown home by Flying Officer Leslie Manser of 50 Squadron, based at RAF Skellingthorpe. Manser was killed when Barte shot out the aircraft's one remaining engine. The British pilot was later awarded the Victoria Cross for keeping the aircraft aloft long enough for his crew to bail out. This is Barte's G9+FM as it appeared in June 1942.

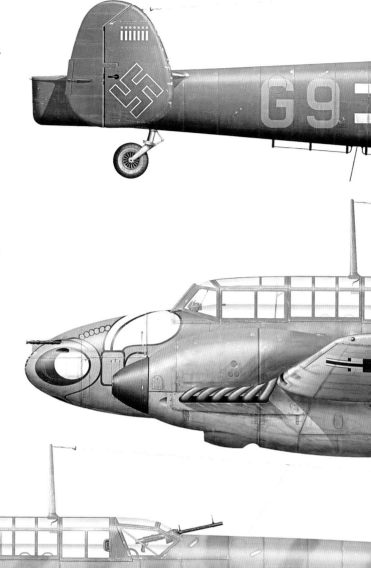

Powered by a pair of DB 605 engines, an initial batch of half a dozen pre-production G-0s were built in June 1942 before full series production began with the G-2 in December 1942 – there was no G-1. Two additional base versions of the Bf 110 G were built – the G-3 long-range reconnaissance version and the G-4 night fighter, which had similar features to the F-4.

However, a huge range of assembly line modifications and depot or unit-installed upgrades resulted in a bewildering variety of Bf 110 G variants. Six of the former, named Umrüst-Bausätz, are known including the U1, which involved the addition of two MG 151/20s to update the G-3's armament, the U5 which was an upgrade of the aircraft's radar to cover a wider search angle and the U6 which installed an electronic system intended to home in on Monica signals emitted by RAF bombers. The U7 was a nitrous oxide power boosting system for the DB 605, the U8 involved fitting additional fuel and oil tanks in the rear cockpit and the U9 saw the four MG17s in the aircraft's upper nose replaced with a pair of MK 108s.

The R1 equipment upgrade was a Rheinmetall-Borsig 37mm cannon mounted in a centreline fuselage gondola, the R2 was another name for the U7, the R3 was the same as the U9, the R4 was both the R2 and R3 fitted together, the R5 was the R1 and R3 together, and R6 was the R1 and R2 together. The R7

Bf 110 E-4

C9+BD of Stab./III./NJG 1, based at Juvincourt, France, December 1942.

Bf 110 G-2

A trio of Soviet Polikarpov R-5s was shot down by Oberfeldwebel Josef Kociok of 10./ZG 1, based at Crimea in the USSR. This is his aircraft, 2N+GU, during the summer of 1943.

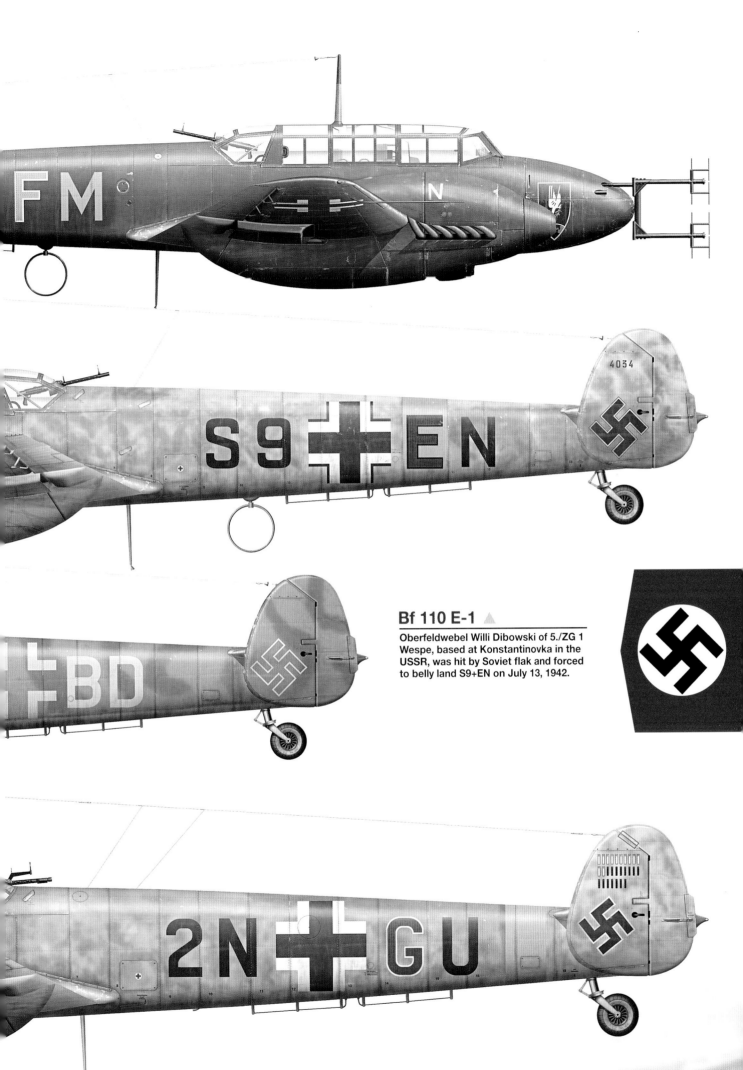

Bf 110 E-1

Oberfeldwebel Willi Dibowski of 5./ZG 1 Wespe, based at Konstantinovka in the USSR, was hit by Soviet flak and forced to belly land S9+EN on July 13, 1942.

LUFTWAFFE FIGHTERS — MESSERSCHMITT BF 110

apparently involved a variation on the usual drop tanks while the R8, otherwise known as Schräge Musik or 'jazz music', saw the Bf 110 G fitted with a pair of upwards firing MG FF/Ms in its rear cockpit. The latter was developed during mid to late 1943 and was introduced on front line machines during mid-1944. Finally, the R9 was another Schräge Musik arrangement but with the more powerful MK 108 fitted instead of the MG FF/Ms.

Beyond the Umrüst-Bausätz modifications and the Rüstsätz upgrades were seven further equipment alterations – the Betriebs and Munition options. There were two of the former – the B1 which saw a streamlined oil tank fitted under the fuselage, and the B2 which involved a pair of underwing 900 litre jettisonable fuel tanks being installed. The M1 saw a tray fitted under the fuselage to hold a pair of MG 151 cannon, the M2 was two ETC 500/IXb bomb racks under the fuselage but covered by a fairing, the M3 was pairs of ETC 50/VIIId racks under the outer wings, M4 was a pair of SD2/XII racks under each outer wing and M5 involved fitting the Bf 110 G with a pair of WrGr. 21 rocket launchers – for firing at bombers. Between December 1942 and April 1945, 797 Bf 110 G-2w, 172 G-3s and 2293 G-4s were built – all together more than half the total number of Bf 110s manufactured.

Remaining in service long after it was declared obsolete, the Bf 110 proved to be an invaluable gun platform for the Luftwaffe – plugging a gap between the highly manoeuvrable but lightweight single-seat fighters and the larger more ponderous bomber and multirole types, such as the Ju 88. ●

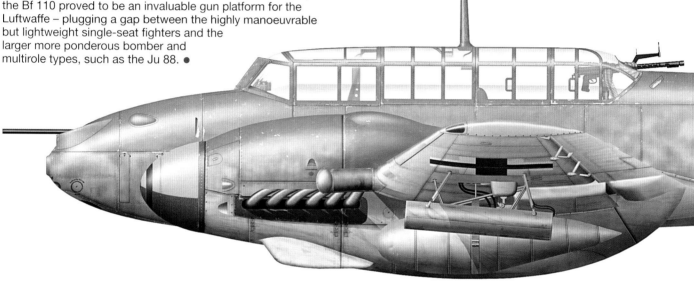

Bf 110 G-2

Black 5 was flown by pilots of 8./ZG 76, based at Öttingen, Germany, during January 1944. It is seen here fitted with WrGr. 21 rocket launchers.

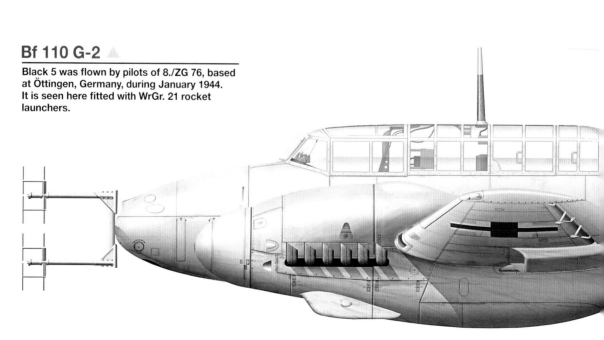

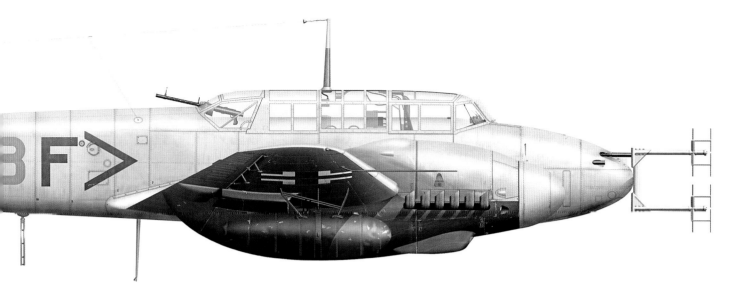

Bf 110 F-4

Chevron 2Z+BF of the Stab./IV./NJG 6, based at Otopeni in Romania during November 1943.

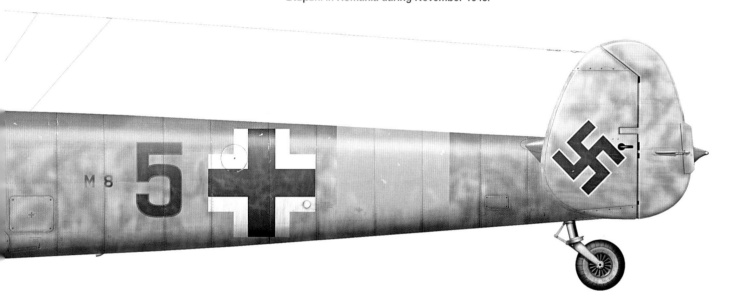

Bf 110 G-4

Night fighter ace Oberleutnant Dietrich Schmidt flew G9+FS on the night of February 11/12, 1944. He was a member of 8./NJG 1, based at Twenthe in Germany. Up to this point, he had shot down eight Lancaster bombers, two Halifaxes, a Wellington and Mosquito.

MESSERSCHMITT BF 110

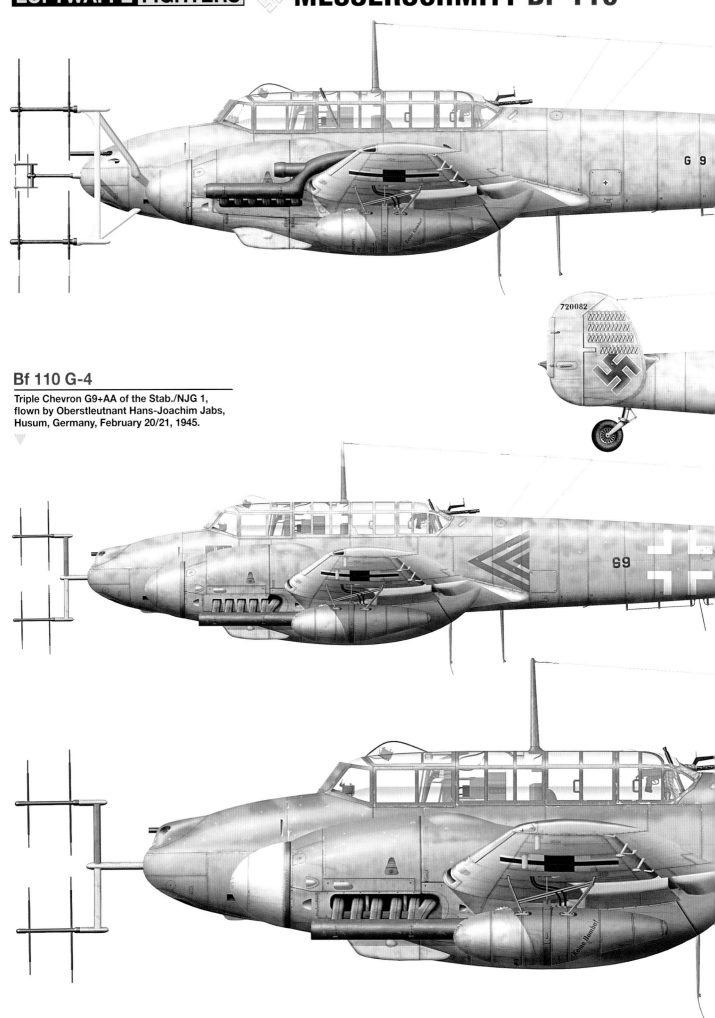

Bf 110 G-4

Triple Chevron G9+AA of the Stab./NJG 1,
flown by Oberstleutnant Hans-Joachim Jabs,
Husum, Germany, February 20/21, 1945.

Bf 110 G-4

G9+WD was the aircraft of night fighter ace Oberleutnant Martin Drewes of Stab./III./NJG 1, stationed at Laon-Athies in France during March 1944. Two months later, on May 22, 1944, he had his most successful mission of the war – shooting down five Lancaster bombers in just over 90 minutes.

Bf 110 G-4

Double Chevron 2Z+MF of Stab IV./NJG 6 flown by Hauptmann Martin 'Tino' Becker, Schleissheim, Germany, November 1944.

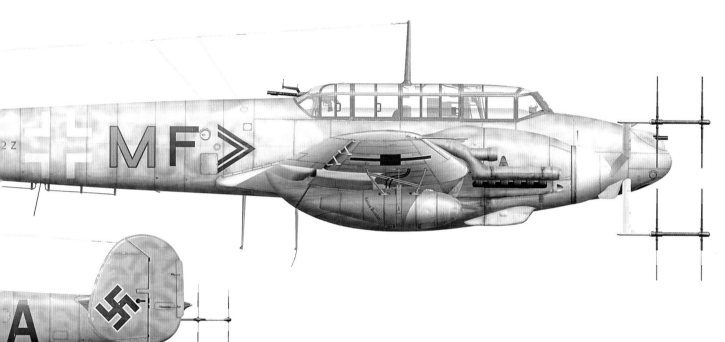

Bf 110 G-4

3C+BA of the Stab./II./NJG 4, flown by Major Heinz-Wolfgang Schnaufer, Eggebek, Germany, April 1945.

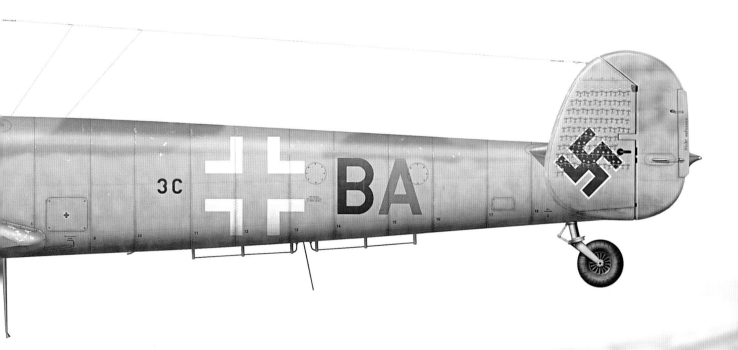

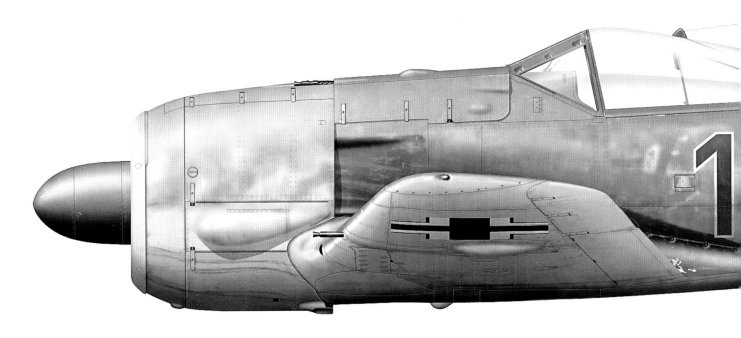

FOCKE-WULF FW 190

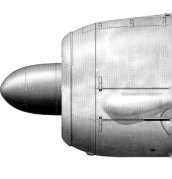

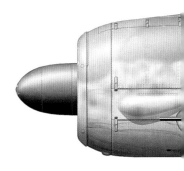

1938-1945

Focke-Wulf's Fw 190 was one of the Luftwaffe's two standard front line day fighters for much of the Second World War, alongside the Messerschmitt Bf 109. In service it earned a reputation for rugged endurance, carrying heavy loads and the ability to out-dive most of its contemporaries. Its large and accommodating airframe was well suited to further development too – enabling Focke-Wulf to use it as the basis for one of the war's most powerful, if short-lived, fighters – the Ta 152.

Focke-Wulf had suffered a disappointing defeat when Messerschmitt's Bf 109 made its Fw 159 design look outdated and clumsy during the 1934-35 contest to produce a modern fighter for the Luftwaffe.

The lightweight Bf 109 was a revelation where the parasol-winged Fw 159 with its complicated hydraulic undercarriage was an embarrassment. However, when the Bf 109 entered service it soon became apparent that its design was far from perfect – its narrow track undercarriage made landing tricky, its heavily glazed cockpit restricted visibility and its small wings reduced its load-carrying capacity.

In 1938, the RLM decided that the Luftwaffe needed a companion for the Bf 109 and Focke-Wulf was perfectly placed to offer up

a design which directly addressed the Messerschmitt's flaws. By now it was also evident that any new fighter would need to be capable of defeating the latest single-seaters being developed elsewhere – particularly the

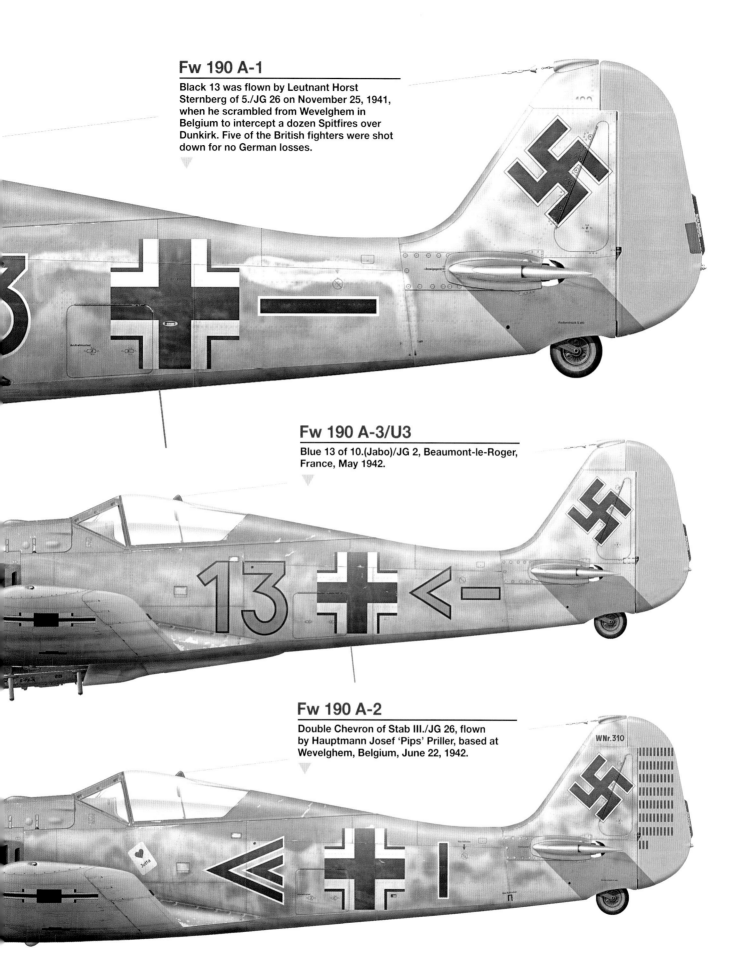

Fw 190 A-1

Black 13 was flown by Leutnant Horst
Sternberg of 5./JG 26 on November 25, 1941,
when he scrambled from Wevelghem in
Belgium to intercept a dozen Spitfires over
Dunkirk. Five of the British fighters were shot
down for no German losses.

Fw 190 A-3/U3

Blue 13 of 10.(Jabo)/JG 2, Beaumont-le-Roger,
France, May 1942.

Fw 190 A-2

Double Chevron of Stab III./JG 26, flown
by Hauptmann Josef 'Pips' Priller, based at
Wevelghem, Belgium, June 22, 1942.

British Supermarine Spitfire.
Therefore, rather than seek to
develop and improve the Fw 159,
Focke-Wulf's chief designer Kurt
Tank decided to begin again with
a blank sheet for what would
become the Fw 190.

He said later: "The
Messerschmitt 109 and the
Spitfire, the two fastest fighters
in the world at the time we began
work on the Fw 190, could both
be summed up as a very large
engine on the front of the smallest

possible airframe; in each case
armament had been added almost
as an afterthought.

"These designs, both of which
admittedly proved successful,
could be likened to racehorses:
given the right amount of

FOCKE-WULF FW 190

Fw 190 A-3

Hauptmann Heinrich Krafft of Stab I/ JG 51 flew Double Chevron from Orel in the USSR during September 1942. Three months later, on December 14, 1942, he survived crash-landing after being hit by flak but was beaten to death by Russian soldiers.

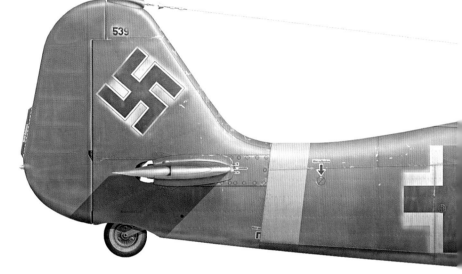

TANK AND HIS TEAM WANTED TO BUILD A FIGHTER THAT WAS TOUGH ENOUGH TO SOAK UP PUNISHMENT

pampering and an easy course, they could outrun almost anything. But the moment the going became tough they were liable to falter.

"During the First World War, I served in the cavalry and in the infantry. I had seen the harsh conditions under which military equipment had to work in wartime. I felt sure that a quite different breed of fighter would also have a place in any future conflict: one that could operate from ill-prepared front line airfields; one that could be flown and maintained by men who had received only a short training; and one that could absorb a reasonable amount of battle damage and still get back.

"This was the background thinking behind the Focke-Wulf 190. It was to be not a 'racehorse'

but a Dienstpferd, a cavalry horse."

Tank and his team wanted to build a fighter that was tough enough to soak up punishment and powerful enough to compete effectively against enemy 'racehorses'. Since superior outright speed was unlikely to be an option, the Focke-Wulf team concentrated on providing heavy firepower, excellent all-round visibility and an advanced powerplant that could suffer battle damage without packing up.

For the latter, Tank gambled on the new 1500hp radial 14-cylinder BMW 139. With two rows of seven cylinders mounted back to back, it generated a lot of heat in a small area but offered a high power to weight ratio. It was to drive a three-bladed 3.4m diameter

Vereingite Deutsche Metallwerke electro-hydraulic variable pitch propeller. Over this was fitted a large Doppelhaube ducted spinner intended to reduce drag.

"So the air-cooled radial engine was fitted to the Fw 190," said Tank. "When the fighter went into action the resilience of this type

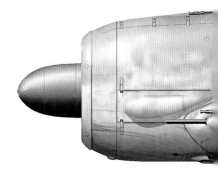

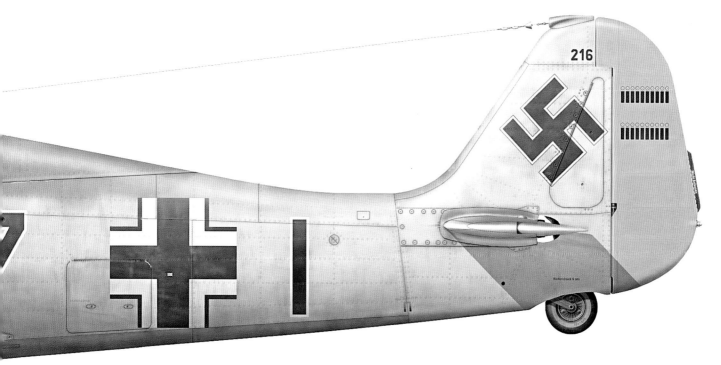

Fw 190 A-2

Oberleutnant Karl Borris of 8./JG 26, one of the key figures involved in testing the earliest Fw 190s, flew Black 7 from Wevelghem, Belgium, on July 30, 1942. That evening at 7.20pm he claimed a Spitfire shot down for his 20th victory.

Fw 190 A-3

Yellow 1 of 6./JG 2, was flown by Oberleutnant Erich Rudorffer on August 19, 1942. Rudorffer, who died in 2016 aged 98, flew more than 1000 combat missions and on one occasion shot down 13 enemy aircraft in 17 minutes.

FOCKE-WULF FW 190

of power plant was proved again and again. There were several occasions when these fighters returned home and made normal landings, having had whole cylinders shot away.

"Once its cooling system had been pierced and the liquid allowed to drain away, the running life of the equivalent liquid-cooled engine would have been about three minutes."

Focke-Wulf submitted the design to the RLM and the company was given the go-ahead to build a mock-up during the autumn of 1938. This was approved and work then began on the Fw 190 V1 prototype. The Focke-Wulf team decided to dispense with engine mounts and had the Fw 190's engine bolted directly to its monocoque fuselage.

Two self-sealing fuel tanks were positioned beneath the pilot – the one below his legs holding 232 litres and the other, under his seat, holding 292 litres – for a total capacity of 524 litres. By comparison, the Bf 109 E had an internal tank capacity of just 250 litres, expandable to 550 litres only with the fitment of a 300 litre drop tank.

The Fw 190's wings, featuring split flaps, were built as a single piece and a series of ridges and corresponding grooves allowed them to be easily fitted into the correct position on the fuselage during assembly. The undercarriage fitted to the first two Fw 190 prototypes was hydraulically operated and although it would rise and lock correctly, it had a tendency to

come loose and hang down slightly during manoeuvres. On later models a more reliable electrically actuated cable system was installed.

Perhaps the Bf 109's greatest design flaw was the way its main wheels retracted outwards into its wings, restricting

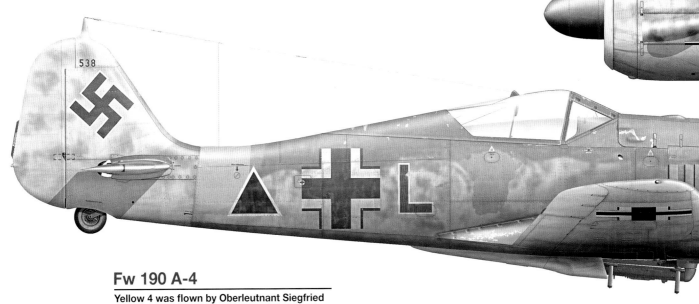

Fw 190 A-4

Yellow 4 was flown by Oberleutnant Siegfried 'Wumm' Schnell of 9./JG 2, based at Théville in France, on February 18, 1943, when he shot down a USAAF aircraft for his 75th victory.

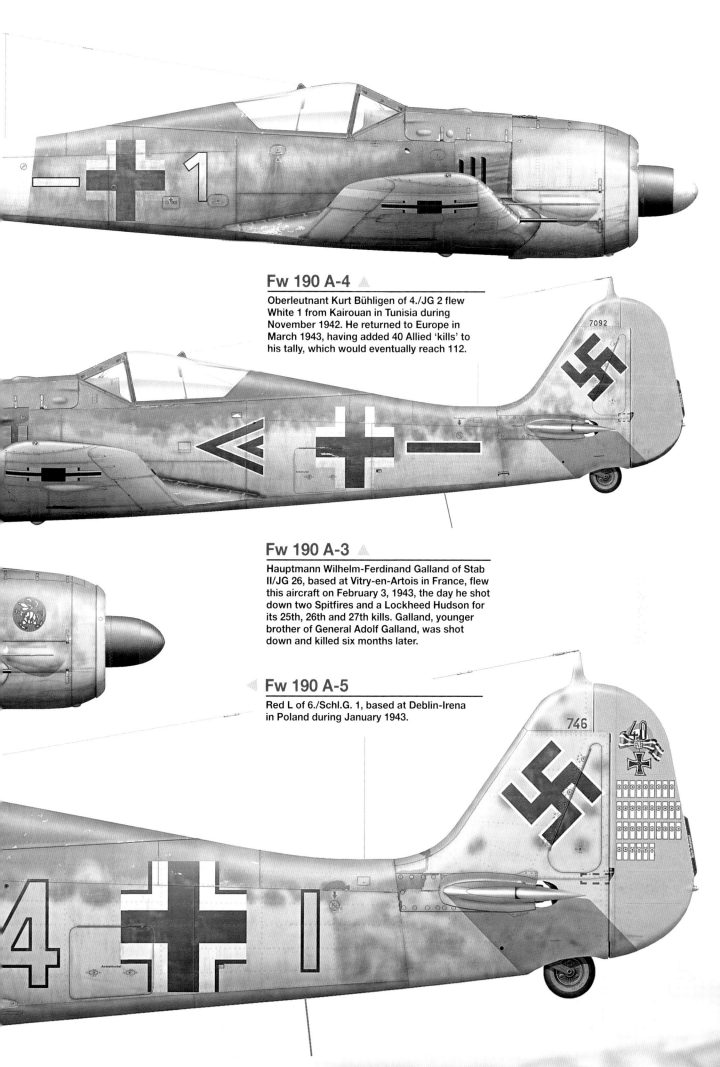

Fw 190 A-4

Oberleutnant Kurt Bühligen of 4./JG 2 flew White 1 from Kairouan in Tunisia during November 1942. He returned to Europe in March 1943, having added 40 Allied 'kills' to his tally, which would eventually reach 112.

Fw 190 A-3

Hauptmann Wilhelm-Ferdinand Galland of Stab II/JG 26, based at Vitry-en-Artois in France, flew this aircraft on February 3, 1943, the day he shot down two Spitfires and a Lockheed Hudson for its 25th, 26th and 27th kills. Galland, younger brother of General Adolf Galland, was shot down and killed six months later.

Fw 190 A-5

Red L of 6./Schl.G. 1, based at Deblin-Irena in Poland during January 1943.

FOCKE-WULF FW 190

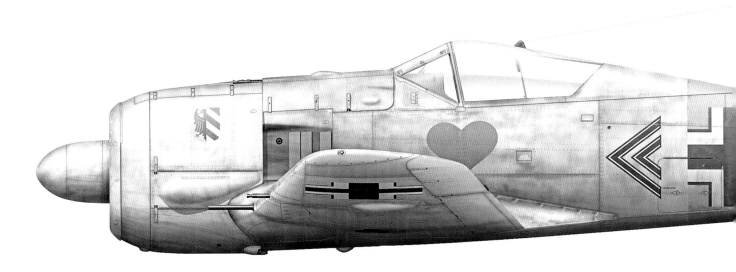

Fw 190 A-4

White 3 was flown by Unteroffizier Karl-Heinz 'Heino' Cordes of 1./JG 54, based at Rijelbitzi in the USSR during the spring of 1943. Cordes survived the war with 62 victories but never received the Knight's Cross of the Iron Cross medal.

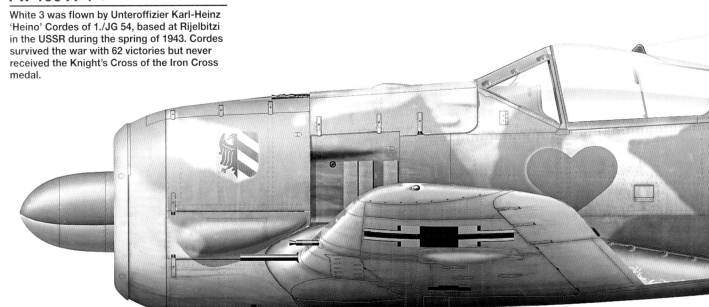

Fw 190 A-5

Hauptmann Fritz Losigkeit, Gruppenkommandeur of I./JG 1 flew this aircraft during April 1943 from Deelen in Holland. On the 17th of the month, he shot down his first B-17 bomber.

Fw 190 A-4

Hauptmann Hans Philipp of Stab I/JG 54 flew this aircraft while based at Staraja-Russa in the USSR during March 1943. He shot down four aircraft on March 17, taking his total to 203 – making him the leading German fighter pilot at the time.

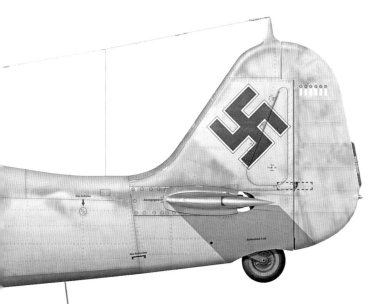

the wing space available for additional weaponry. Focke-Wulf therefore designed the Fw 190's wide track undercarriage so that the main wheels retracted into the underside of the fuselage – leaving the wings uncluttered.

The first armament arrangement to be fitted was two machine guns and two cannon – a 7.9mm MG 17 with 800 rounds and a 20mm MG 151 with 160 rounds in each wing, close to the fuselage. For ease of maintenance, large access panels were provided and those components that would require the most frequent serving were placed within easy reach.

A small retractable ladder was provided on the lower edge of the fuselage on the port side, aft of the wing root, along with a spring-loaded handhold and another step to reach the cockpit. Once aboard, the pilot sat in a semi-reclined seat that was vertically adjustable over a range of 4in. The flight instruments were laid out in what was intended to be a logical way and internal systems received a 24v power supply from a 1000W generator.

Work on building the Fw 190 V1 was coordinated by Tank's assistant Willi Käther, with engineer Rudolf Blaser designing the structure and test pilots Hans Sander and Kurt Melhorn

THE FIRST ARMAMENT ARRANGEMENT TO BE FITTED WAS TWO MACHINE GUNS AND TWO CANNON

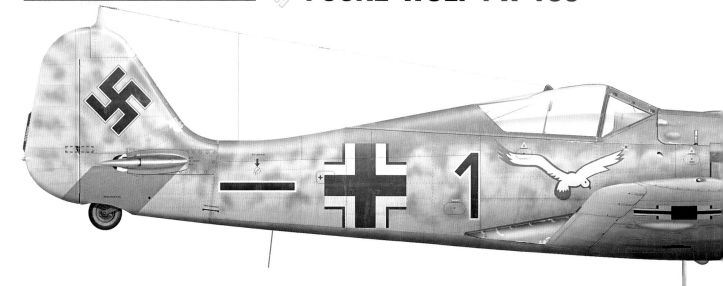

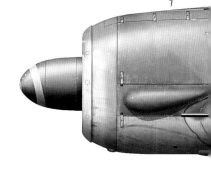

both contributing ideas and suggestions from an early stage.

Sander took the finished product, given the civil registration D-OPZE, up for its first flight on June 1, 1939, and though he was impressed by its performance he found it difficult to fly for another reason: "For the first flight, I wore only a thin flying suit over my normal underwear, socks, ordinary shoes, and a flying helmet with my oxygen mask hanging loose, yet soon after take-off I began to sweat profusely.

"The rear of the engine was hard up against the front wall of the cockpit, and my feet and rudder pedals were either side of the engine accessories. The temperature in the cockpit rose to 55^{0}C. I felt as though I was sitting with my feet in the fire. The heat was bearable but ever since I have had some sympathy for a steak on a grill."

It may have been hanging loose at first, but Sander soon had to put his oxygen mask on as engine exhaust fumes began to seep into the cockpit through the canopy's unsealed edges. It had been expected that the BMW 139 would get hot during operation but exactly how hot had been badly underestimated. Nevertheless, the Fw 190 showed great promise. Later tests determined that the V1's overheating was being caused at least in part by the Doppelhaube spinner, but this was retained for aerodynamic reasons.

Just over a month later, on July 3, 1939, the as-yet unarmed V1 was demonstrated for Adolf Hitler, Hermann Göring, Ernst Udet, Erhart Milch and General Wilhelm Keitel. The fully-armed Fw 190 V2, FO+LZ, made its first flight on October 31, 1939, equipped with a FuG VII radio and Revi

C/12c gunsight in addition to its weapons.

Following on from the company tradition established by the Stieglitz, Stösser, Weihe and the rest, it was at this time that the Fw 190 was given its 'bird name' – Würger (Shrike). This appeared on company brochures but does not appear to have been more widely adopted.

Overheating problems persisted and the V2 was experimentally fitted with a new 10-bladed cooling fan under its spinner, but this did little to alleviate the issue. Attention was now focused on the spinner, with BMW arguing that it diverted cool air away from the engine. Focke-Wulf tried it without the Doppelhaube – and discovered that the spinner had actually served to reduce the aircraft's top speed by 12mph, rather than enhancing it.

The firm had failed to account for the inch-wide gap between the spinner and the leading edge of the engine cowling, which sucked in air and created drag. With the spinner scrapped, a NACA-style engine cowling was adopted. Göring was given a personal demonstration of the newly reconfigured V2 and an order for 40 pre-production Fw 190 A-0 aircraft was placed.

Removing the spinner did not solve the BMW 139's overheating problem, however. The engine manufacturer was finally forced to concede that it was incurable and 139 production was halted after just 47 units had been made. Fortunately, BMW had been working on another design in parallel – the 801.

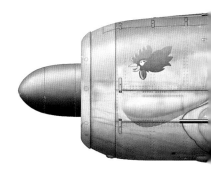

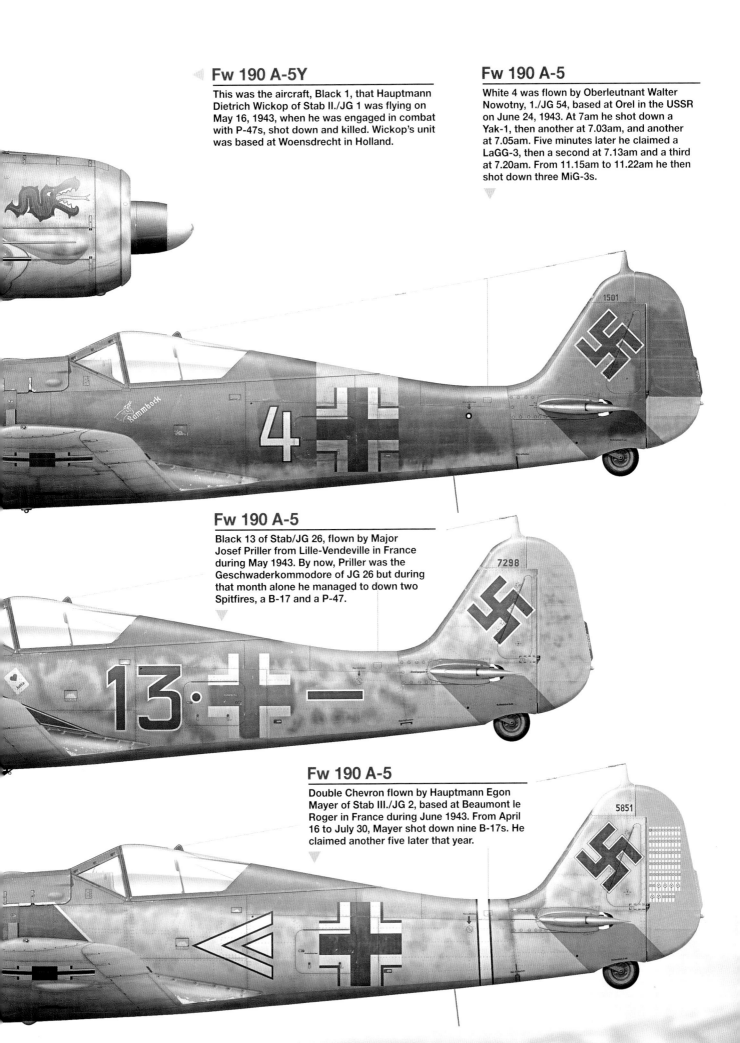

Fw 190 A-5Y

This was the aircraft, Black 1, that Hauptmann Dietrich Wickop of Stab II./JG 1 was flying on May 16, 1943, when he was engaged in combat with P-47s, shot down and killed. Wickop's unit was based at Woensdrecht in Holland.

Fw 190 A-5

White 4 was flown by Oberleutnant Walter Nowotny, 1./JG 54, based at Orel in the USSR on June 24, 1943. At 7am he shot down a Yak-1, then another at 7.03am, and another at 7.05am. Five minutes later he claimed a LaGG-3, then a second at 7.13am and a third at 7.20am. From 11.15am to 11.22am he then shot down three MiG-3s.

Fw 190 A-5

Black 13 of Stab/JG 26, flown by Major Josef Priller from Lille-Vendeville in France during May 1943. By now, Priller was the Geschwaderkommodore of JG 26 but during that month alone he managed to down two Spitfires, a B-17 and a P-47.

Fw 190 A-5

Double Chevron flown by Hauptmann Egon Mayer of Stab III./JG 2, based at Beaumont le Roger in France during June 1943. From April 16 to July 30, Mayer shot down nine B-17s. He claimed another five later that year.

FOCKE WULF FW 190

This incorporated elements of both the BMW 139 and a design produced by Bramo, the 329. BMW had absorbed this smaller rival company in 1939 and was able to utilise the technology it had developed on several of its own designs.

The BMW 801 had a built-in cooling fan and was already proving to be both powerful and reliable. It had nearly the same diameter as the BMW 139 but was slightly longer and heavier.

Meanwhile, the V2, re-registered as RM+CB, was damaged in an accident on March 2, 1940, when it flipped over onto its back during taxying. Repaired, it was used for weapons trials starting in September 1940. V1 was taken to Rechlin for further flight trials on June 11, 1940. Work on Fw 190 V3 and V4, which were nearing completion with fittings prepared for the 139, was halted. The V3 was cannibalised for spares and the V4 was destroyed during load tests.

With the BMW 801 came another innovation – the Kommandogeräte engine management mechanism. This automated the adjustment of manifold pressure, compressor gearshift, fuel mixture regulation,

ignition control and constant speed control through propeller pitch.

The first BMW 801-equipped Fw 190 was the V5, which made its maiden flight during April 1940. This featured a strengthened airframe and uprated undercarriage struts to cope with the additional 150kg weight of the new engine. The cockpit was moved

back to allow for the longer engine and the aircraft's overall length increased from 8.73m to 8.798m. This offered two benefits – the cockpit was now cooler, being a little further away from the engine, and there was now sufficient room to fit a pair of machine guns onto the nose if required.

> **THE AIRCRAFT'S OVERALL LENGTH INCREASED, MEANING THE COCKPIT WAS COOLER AND A PAIR OF MACHINE GUNS COULD BE PUT INTO THE NOSE IF REQUIRED**

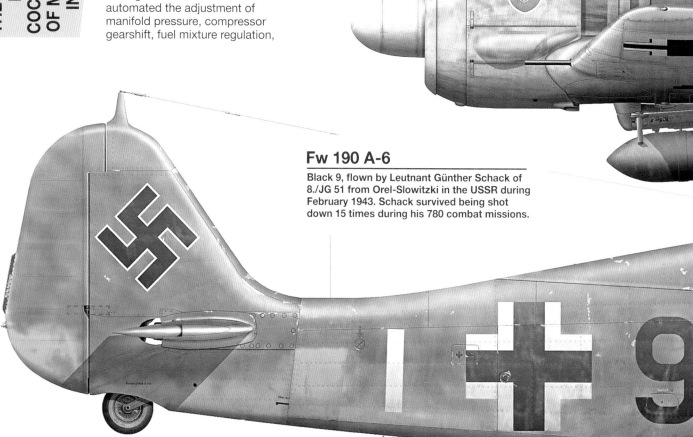

Fw 190 A-6

Black 9, flown by Leutnant Günther Schack of 8./JG 51 from Orel-Slowitzki in the USSR during February 1943. Schack survived being shot down 15 times during his 780 combat missions.

Fw 190 A-4/U8

One of the more unusual episodes of the Second World War was on April 16, 1943, when Feldwebel Otto Bechtold of 3./SKG 10, based at Poix in France, and three of his comrades got lost in dense fog and, thinking they were over France, attempted landings at RAF West Malling in Kent. Only Bechtold's Fw 190, Yellow H, survived intact.

Fw 190 A-4

This Double Chevron aircraft was flown by Oberleutnant Fritz Schröter of Stab III./SKG 10 from La Fauconnerie airfield in Tunisia during March 1943.

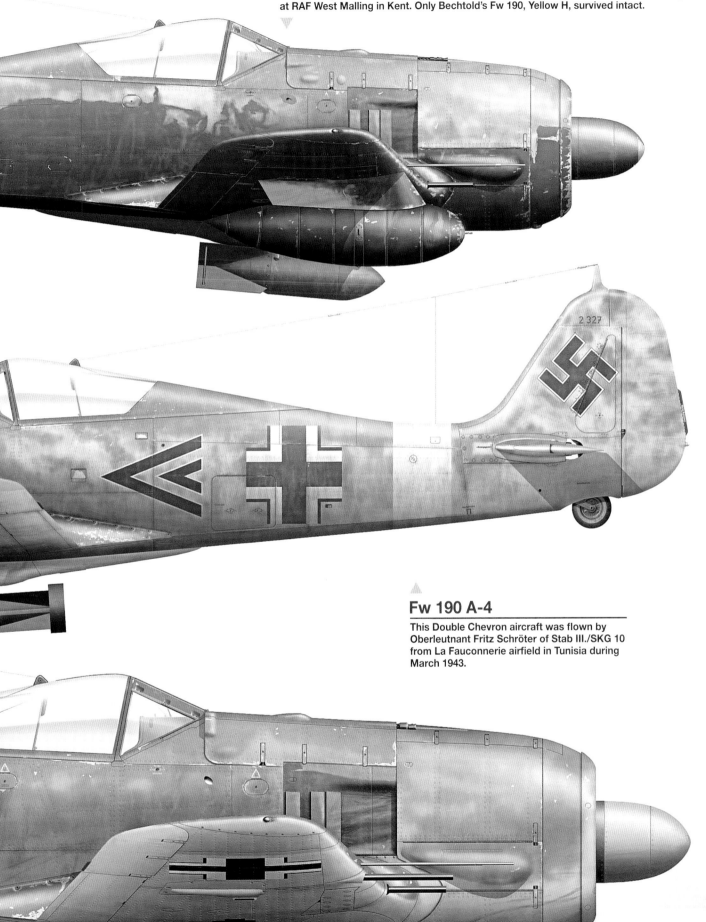

FOCKE-WULF FW 190

Fw 190 A-5Y

Unteroffizier Bernhard Kunze of 1./JG 1, based at Deelen, Holland, was flying White 1 at 7.43pm on August 19, 1943, when he shot down a B-17 near Haamstede.

Another issue thrown up during testing was the ineffectiveness of the aircraft's emergency canopy release mechanism. The aerodynamic form of the canopy was so good that above 270mph pilots were unable to get it open due to the air flowing over it. Various means to overcome this were tried – including a bungee cord and compressed air – but everything failed. Tests determined

that the canopy would not open for anything less than the equivalent of 50hp, so Blaser built a mechanism which used a 20mm explosive cartridge to push a piston which in turn punched the canopy rearwards to the point where the airflow caught it and whipped it away from the airframe.

Sander, who was also a qualified engineer, was inspired by this invention to come up with

a primitive ejection seat mechanism for the Fw 190 but it was found that the explosive charges available were insufficient to propel the pilot away from the aircraft's tail, so the idea was abandoned.

FW 190 A-0 TO A-9

With its heavier BMW 801 lump the Fw 190 V5 had a higher wing

Fw 190 A-5

The brightly coloured personal aircraft of Major Hermann Graf, commander of fighter pilot school Ergänzungs-Jagdgruppe Ost based at Toulouse-Blagnac, France. He shot down a pair of B-17s on September 6, 1943.

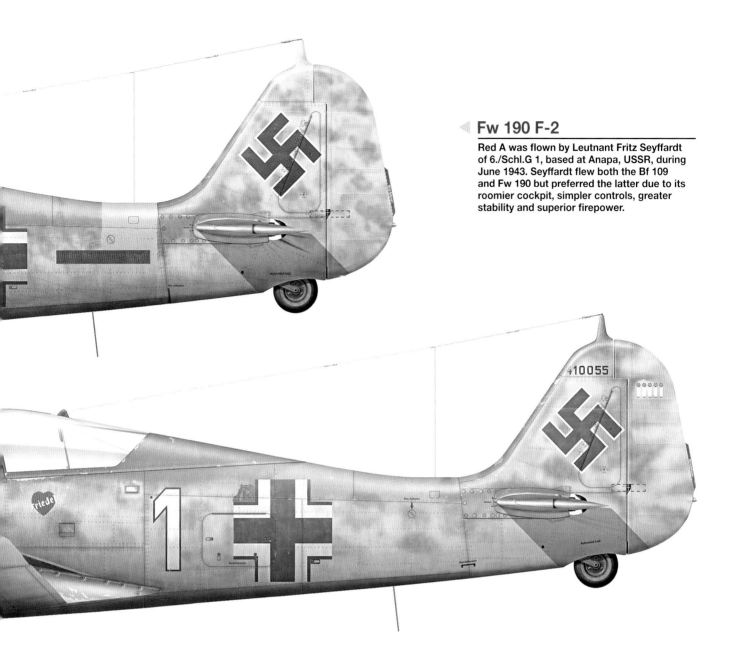

Fw 190 F-2

Red A was flown by Leutnant Fritz Seyffardt of 6./Schl.G 1, based at Anapa, USSR, during June 1943. Seyffardt flew both the Bf 109 and Fw 190 but preferred the latter due to its roomier cockpit, simpler controls, greater stability and superior firepower.

loading and handling suffered – so it was decided that longer wings were needed. Meanwhile, the Fw 190 V6 was completed and took its first flight on May 31, 1940, but its BMW 801 proved to be faulty and had to be swapped for a new one after only nine flights. Both the V5 and V6 were armed with a quartet of 7.9mm MG 17 machine guns – two in the wing roots and two on the nose.

This configuration was retrospectively referred to as the Fw 190 A-0/U1. The 'U' stood for 'Umrüst bausatz' or 'conversion kit' – an 'Umbau' was a change to the aircraft's configuration that could only be carried out at the factory or on rare occasions in the field by an approved Focke-Wulf subcontractor.

A series of nine more A-0s were then produced, taking their first

flights between July and October 1940 and being used to test various different weapons layouts, engine modifications and other alterations to the aircraft's design. All of these had the original small wing that had been a feature since the V1.

Finally, on October 10, 1940, Fw 190 A-0 WNr. 0016 (the 16th Fw 190 built after the six 'Versuchs' aircraft and the nine A-0s), coded

Fw 190 A-5

Having shot down 50 Supermarine Spitfires and 16 other Allied aircraft between September 1940 and November 1942, Oberleutnant Josef Wurmheller of 9./JG 2 based at Vannes, France, switched his attention to B-17s – destroying 11 of them up to the time of this aircraft, Yellow 2, in September 1943.

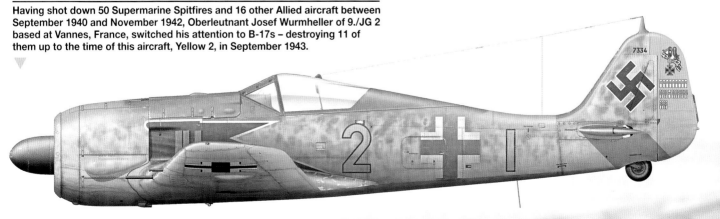

KB+PR, made its flying debut with an enlarged wing. Each wingtip had been extended by just over 50cm, giving it a wingspan of 10.5m, compared to 9.5m of all the earlier examples. Wing area was correspondingly increased from 14.9sq m to 18.3sq m.

The amount the wing tapered was also reduced so that the wingtip itself took on a squarer look. In later versions of the Fw 190, the tailplane area was also increased. Performance was still worse than the small-wing BMW 139 Fw 190s however, with top speed at 18,372ft down to 426mph from 432mph and range down to 671 miles from 684 miles. Service ceiling was improved though, from 36,090ft to 37,400ft.

The new wing was thereafter referred to as the V5g and Fw 190s without it were V5ks, the 'g' being for 'grosser' (larger) and the 'k' being for 'kleiner' (smaller), and was installed on all subsequent Fw 190 A aircraft.

A total of 29 Fw 190 A-0s were built, not including the V1, V2, V5 and V6 prototypes. They were fitted with either the BMW 801 C-0 or C-1 and had shorter spinners than later models, differently shaped armoured cowling rings and symmetrical teardrop-shaped bulges on the engine cowling to cover the interior air intakes for the engine. There were no cooling slots aft of the exhaust pipes on the sides of the aircraft either. The last A-0 was completed in October 1941.

In early 1941, WNr. 0007 became the prototype for the Fw 190 A-1 and was given the new production WNr. 190.0110.001. The 190 was the type, the 011 meant 'A-1', the 0 was the manufacturer – Focke-Wulf – and the 001 was the individual aircraft's serial number. Other companies that later built the Fw 190 had their own numbers where Focke-Wulf had the 0. Ago had 2, Arado had 5 and 6 and Fieseler had 7.

As the template for the front line fighters that were to follow, WNr. 190.0110.001 had a BMW 801 C-1 engine generating 1560hp at sea level, a pair of MG 17s over the engine and two more in the wing roots. There was also provision for the fitment of two 20mm cannon in outer wing positions.

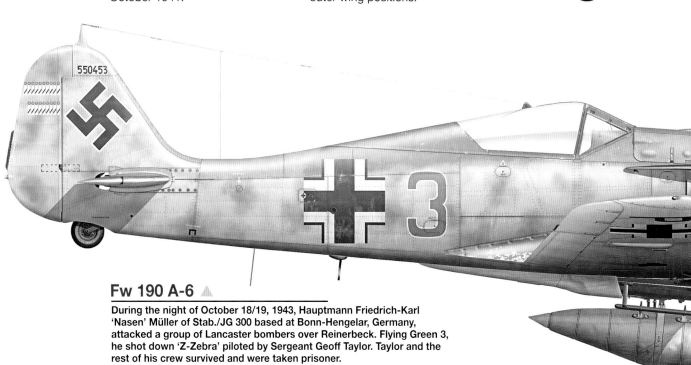

Fw 190 A-6

During the night of October 18/19, 1943, Hauptmann Friedrich-Karl 'Nasen' Müller of Stab./JG 300 based at Bonn-Hengelar, Germany, attacked a group of Lancaster bombers over Reinerbeck. Flying Green 3, he shot down 'Z-Zebra' piloted by Sergeant Geoff Taylor. Taylor and the rest of his crew survived and were taken prisoner.

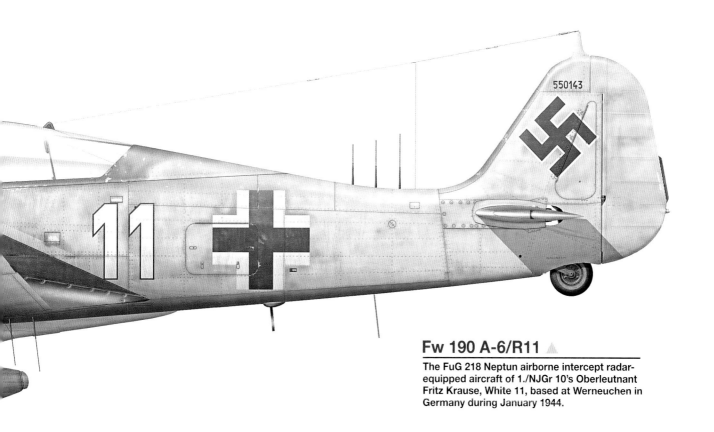

Fw 190 A-6/R11

The FuG 218 Neptun airborne intercept radar-equipped aircraft of 1./NJGr 10's Oberleutnant Fritz Krause, White 11, based at Werneuchen in Germany during January 1944.

Fw 190 A-6/R11

Night fighter Red 21 was flown by pilots of 1./NJGr 10, based at Le Bourget, France, during February 1944.

The II. Gruppe of Jagdgeschwader 26 (II./JG 26) was the first Luftwaffe unit to convert to the Fw 190. In March 1941, JG 26 officers Oblt Otto Behrens and Lt Karl Borris were seconded to establish and lead an experimental unit, Erprobungsstaffel 190, at Rechlin-Roggenthin to ready the Fw 190 for active service with the Luftwaffe. Both men had technical backgrounds and they were given a team of 30 ground crew and half a dozen A-0s to work with.

Borris found the Fw 190 robust and capable but had ongoing problems with its BMW 801 C-1 engine. He said: "Whatever could possibly go wrong with it did. We hardly dared to leave the immediate vicinity of the airfield with our six prototype machines.

"Oil lines ruptured. The heavily armoured oil cooler ring in front of the engine often broke. The bottom cylinder of the rear row seized again and again, since the oil pump and the cooling surfaces were too small. Leaking fuel lines left the pilots in a dazed state from the fumes, unable to climb out of their aeroplanes unaided."

FOCKE-WULF FW 190

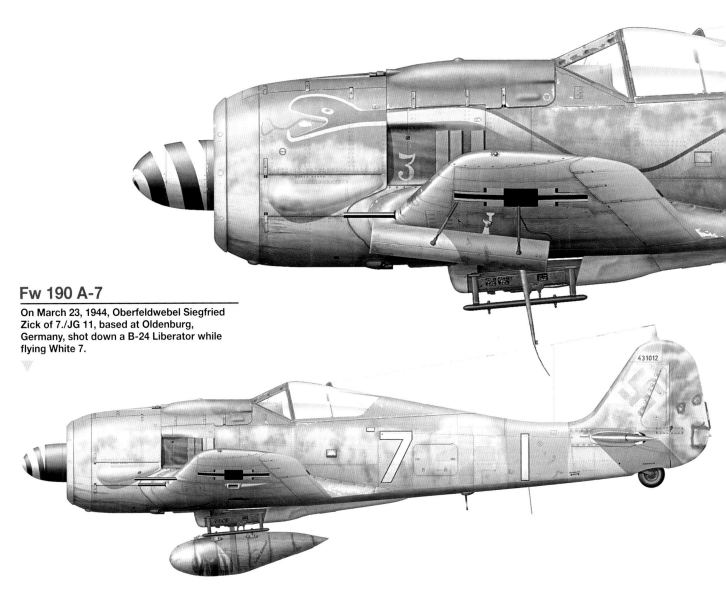

Fw 190 A-7

On March 23, 1944, Oberfeldwebel Siegfried Zick of 7./JG 11, based at Oldenburg, Germany, shot down a B-24 Liberator while flying White 7.

By this time much of the Luftwaffe's strength was being drawn away east to prepare for Operation Barbarossa – the invasion of the Soviet Union. By June 28, 1941, there were just two complete Jagdgeschwader (fighter wings) left in the west – JG 2 and 26. Between them they could field a total of 140 serviceable Messerschmitt Bf 109Es and Fs.

In July 1941, despite the engine difficulties, Behrens and Borris' unit was moved Le Bourget airfield near Paris to begin the conversion training of II./JG 26. It was a slow process – two of the new fighters were lost on August 7 when they suffered engine failure and crashed, another on August 9. BMW was reluctant to take responsibility and was struggling to make the latest development in the series, the BMW 801 D, ready for service.

The biggest problem the company faced was a lack of high quality metals which could be used

to create heat-resistant alloys. Engines frequently suffered severe heat damage after just a few hours in operation, necessitating a complete rebuild or replacement.

Nevertheless, by the end of August the whole of II./JG 26 was working up on the Fw 190 and by October, III./JG 26 based at Coquelles, near Calais, had also begun converting to the Fw 190. It was this unit's technical officer, Oblt Rolf Schödter, who finally found a workable solution to the BMW engine's overheating problems. After the usual round of failures suffered by the engines of III./JG 26's Fw 190s, Schödter collected up all the failed units and had them sent to his repair shop.

Examining all the failed engines together enabled Schödter's team to quickly identify the source of the problem. It was determined that the exhaust system was to blame and simply rerouting it reduced the temperature of the bottom cylinder of the rear row – thereby removing

the single greatest source of engine failure on the Fw 190.

Schödter's 'quick fix' was adopted as a factory modification and soon BMW 801 C and later D units could run for more than 100 hours without suffering crippling heat damage.

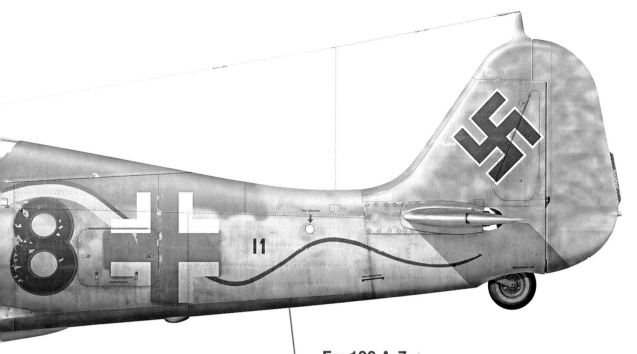

Fw 190 A-7

Black 8, flown by Unteroffizier Walter Gerlach of 3./JG 10, based at Delitzsch in Germany, February 14, 1944.

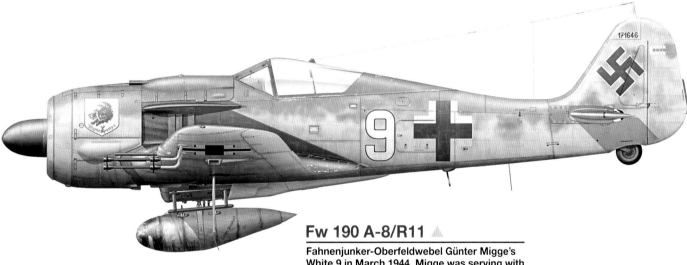

Fw 190 A-8/R11

Fahnenjunker-Oberfeldwebel Günter Migge's White 9 in March 1944. Migge was serving with 1./NJGr 10, based at Werneuchen in Germany.

Fw 190 A-7

Eighth Air Force bombers attacking Focke-Wulf and Junkers factories on April 11, 1944, were set upon by the fighters of JG 1, stationed at Twente in Holland. Major Emil-Rudolf Schnoor, flying White 20, shot down two B-17s.

FOCKE-WULF FW 190

From June 1941 to May 1942, Focke-Wulf built a total of 102 Fw 190 A-1 fighters. They each had a new longer spinner and the cowling bulges over the engine air intakes became asymmetrical – a feature that would remain for the rest of the A-series. The exhaust panels on either side of the aircraft remained unslotted, although some aircraft later had slots retrofitted.

The A-1 saw the introduction of the cartridge-fired cockpit canopy emergency opening system and the pilot's head armour was a different shape from that of the A-0.

The next major upgrade, the Fw 190 A-2, was to be mass produced by subcontractors Arado at Warnemünde and AGO at Oschersleben. It differed from the A-1 in having the BMW 801 C-2, rather than the C-1, and its weaponry was updated to replace the wing-root MG 17s with MG 151 cannon. Ventilation slots were fitted to the exhaust panels on the sides of the fuselage as standard to further aid cooling. A total of 426 were produced up to August 1942.

The A-3 was introduced to incorporate the BMW 801 D-2 and included the exhaust re-routing devised by Schödter. Focke-Wulf

Fw 190 A-6

During his time in command of III./JG 11, Major Anton Hackl shot down 25 four-engined bombers. This aircraft is his Double Chevron as it appeared on April 15, 1944, when the unit was based at Oldenburg in Germany.

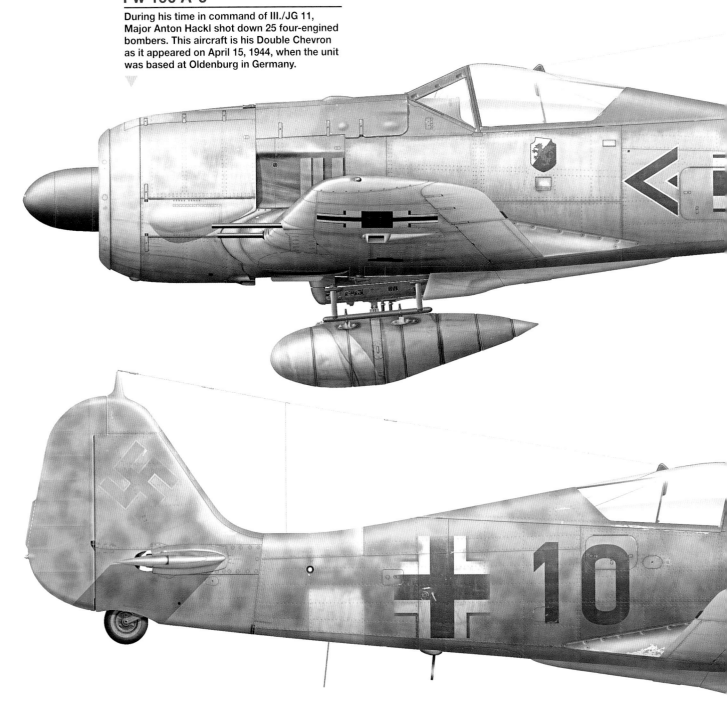

built the first batch of three A-3s in November 1941 and had turned out 74 by the end of March 1942, while simultaneously continuing to build Fw 190 A-2s. Arado and AGO both began A-3 production in April 1942 and in May were joined by a third company, Fieseler, which built its first A-3 that month. Also that month, a third Jagdgeschwader, JG 1, began converting to the Fw 190. II./JG 1 based at

Woensdrecht and Katwijk in Holland began receiving A-2s and A-3s on May 12, 1942. A total of 509 A-3s were constructed. A-2s and A-3s are perhaps the most difficult Fw 190s to tell apart.

By now it was readily apparent to front line Luftwaffe units that the rapid increase in Fw 190 production had resulted in corners being cut and by mid-May the RLM had had enough of poorly

finished and faulty aircraft being delivered to front line units.

It called two meetings, first with BMW on May 22 and then with Focke-Wulf on May 27, to demand that the situation be improved and the issues with build quality resolved.

A list of 24 complaints about the Fw 190s being delivered had been compiled by JG 26 technical officer Ernst Battmer. Among

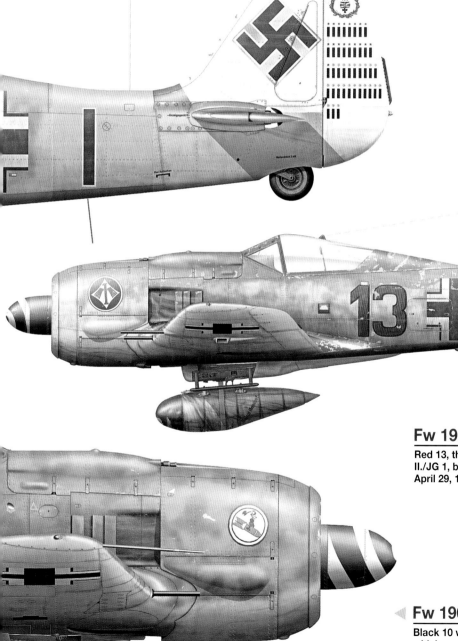

Fw 190 A-7

Red 13, the aircraft of Major Heinz Bär, Stab II./JG 1, based at Störmende, Germany, on April 29, 1944.

Fw 190 F-8

Black 10 was flown by pilots of 2./SG 4, which was based at Rieti in central Italy during May 1944.

Fw 190 A-8/R2 ▲

Yellow 2 flown by Unteroffizier Walter Uecker
of 9./JG 54, on May 19, 1944.

the problems he listed were irregularly sized wings made by contractors, poor wheel brakes, fuel pump failures, over-large control sticks, weak undercarriage bolts, leaky valves, poorly fitting cockpit canopies, too-short starter handles, woeful external paint finish and frequent engine failures.

This report was sent to Focke-Wulf's design team as a follow-on from the meeting and they quickly set to work rectifying each issue. Around a third of the problems identified by Battmer were cured in the Fw 190 A-4, which kept the BMW 801 D-2 engine but with provision for GM-1 nitrous oxide injection and production of it began in July 1942 at Fieseler

and Arado. Armament remained the same – two nose mounted MG 17 machine guns, two MG 151 cannon in the wing roots and two MG FF cannon in the outer wing positions – but the big change was a new radio set, the FuG 16 Z, replacing previous models' FuG VIIa. This required a small radio mast to be fitted atop the tail fin and made it easy to distinguish an A-4 from its predecessors since none of them had it.

Some A-4s were also fitted with controllable cooling vents on the fuselage sides in place of the ordinary slots. Production of the A-4 ceased at Focke-Wulf in November 1942 and at Fieseler in February 1943. It was dropped

from the Arado production line in June 1943 and AGO continued to produce it until August 1943. A total of 896 A-4s were constructed.

Nearly all of the 24 complaints were addressed in the A-5, which entered production in November 1942 at Focke-Wulf's own factories – Arado, AGO and Fieseler introduced it later. It was similar to the A-4 in most respects but had a 6¼in section inserted between the rearward edge of the engine cowling and the fuselage – moving the engine further away from the cockpit and further improving the BMW 801's cooling.

With this new longer nose, the A-5's length was 29ft 4½in compared to the A-4's 28ft

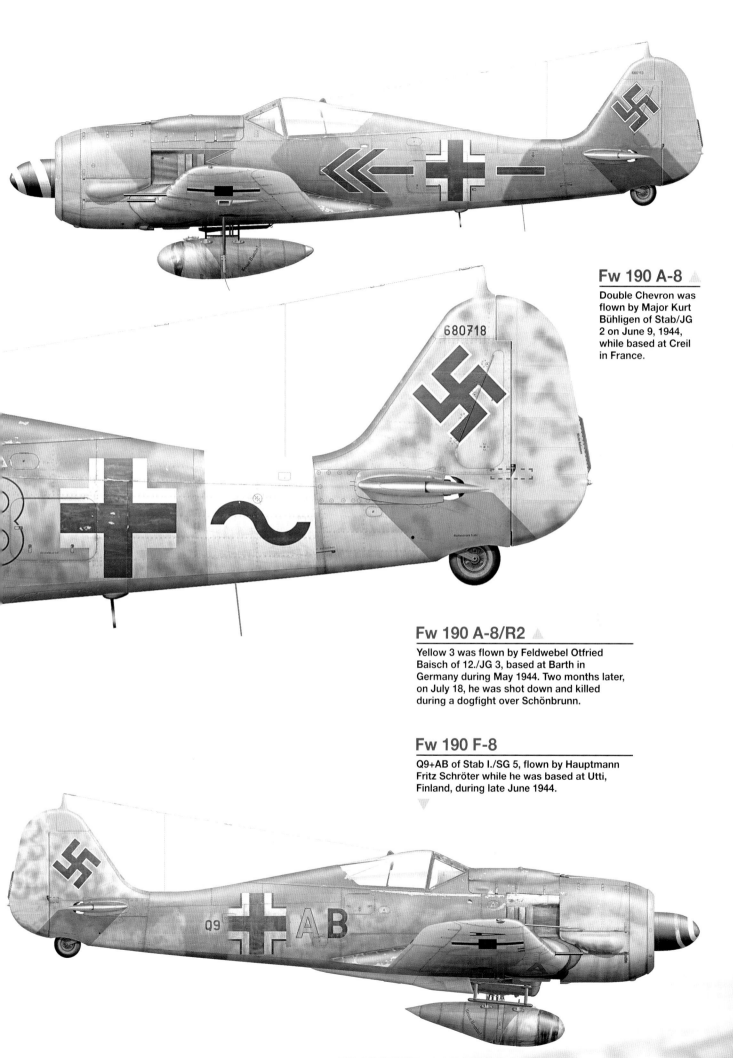

Fw 190 A-8 ▲

Double Chevron was flown by Major Kurt Bühligen of Stab/JG 2 on June 9, 1944, while based at Creil in France.

Fw 190 A-8/R2 ▲

Yellow 3 was flown by Feldwebel Otfried Baisch of 12./JG 3, based at Barth in Germany during May 1944. Two months later, on July 18, he was shot down and killed during a dogfight over Schönbrunn.

Fw 190 F-8

Q9+AB of Stab I./SG 5, flown by Hauptmann Fritz Schröter while he was based at Utti, Finland, during late June 1944.

FOCKE-WULF FW 190

9½in. The A-5 also got updated instrumentation in the cockpit and an Eka 16 gun camera. Shifting the engine further forward also altered the aircraft's centre of gravity and enabled it to carry additional weight further aft. The A-5 kept the standard A-2 to A-4 armament but there were a wide range of Umbau factory-fit modifications and Rüstsatz field conversion kits produced which took full advantage of the aircraft's ability to carry a greater ordnance load. The A-5 was built alongside the F-2 and G-2 versions of the Fw 190, which has resulted in confusion over precisely how many were built. The combined total of all three was 1863 up to August 1943

when AGO finally stopped building them.

The first A-6 was produced by AGO in April 1943 and the type was built exclusively by Focke-Wulf's subcontractors, with the company itself producing none. The main difference from the A-5 was the replacement of the MG FF cannon in the outer wing positions with two more MG 151s. This meant armament was now two MG 17s on the aircraft's nose, two MG 151s in the wing roots and two more in the outer wings. The bulkier MG 151 required a bulge on the upper surface of the A-6's wing as well as the bulge which had already been required on the

lower surface to accommodate the MG FF. In addition, the MG 151's longer barrel protruded further from the wing's leading edge – another visual identifier.

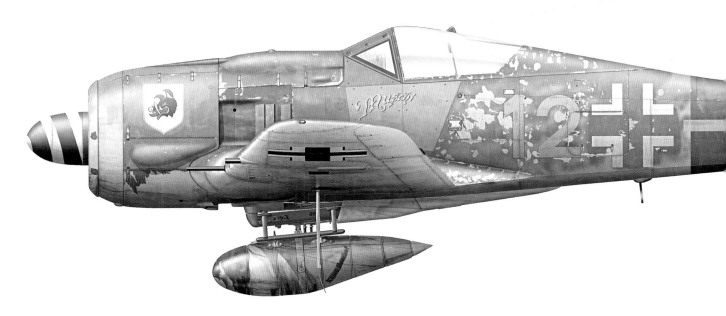

Fw 190 A-8/R2

Leutnant Hans Weik of 10./JG 3, based at Memmingen, Germany, flew White 7 on July 7, 1944 – the day he achieved his penultimate victory – a B-24 Liberator. Eleven days later he shot down a B-17 but was forced to bail out and suffered serious shoulder and arm injuries which effectively put him out of action for the rest of the war.

Fw 190 A-8

Red 19 was the regular aircraft of Unteroffizier Ernst Schröder of 5./JG 300, based at Löbnitz, Germany, during August 1944.

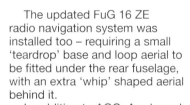

Fw 190 A-8/R2

Unteroffizier Paul Lixfeld of 6./JG 300's battered Yellow 12 as it appeared at Löbnitz, Germany, in November 1944. The boar's head badge on the cowling dates from the Gruppe's days as a 'Wilde Sau' unit. The significance of 'Muschi' is unknown.

The updated FuG 16 ZE radio navigation system was installed too – requiring a small 'teardrop' base and loop aerial to be fitted under the rear fuselage, with an extra 'whip' shaped aerial behind it.

In addition to AGO, Arado and Fieseler, a fourth subcontractor built a small number of Fw 190 A-6s – 20 being completed by Norddeutsche Dornier as Wismar. When production ceased in February 1944, a total of 1137 had been built.

The introduction of the Fw 190 A-7 in November 1943 saw a further armament upgrade – the two nose-mounted MG 17 7.9mm machine guns finally being replaced with higher calibre 13mm MG 131s. These were about the same length but weighed more and had a lower rate of fire at 900rpm compared to 1200 for the MG 17. The A-7 also received an upgraded gunsight, with the Revi C/12d being replaced by the Revi 16b, and the tailwheel was enlarged from 13.8 x 5.3in to 15

x 6in. The A-7 had the briefest production run of any Fw 190 A type – the last examples being built in March 1944, just five months after the first. It was manufactured by Focke-Wulf (150), AGO (270) and Fieseler (200), with Arado out of the picture, being still heavily engaged in building the A-6 up to February 1944. A total of 620 were made.

The Fw 190 A-8 was the version built in the greatest numbers and is widely regarded as the 'definitive' 190. It differed from the A-7 in having an additional 115 litre fuel tank fitted in the rear fuselage to improve range without the need to always carry a drop tank. This meant that the radio had to be relocated to just behind the pilot's seat. It was also upgraded from the FuG 16 Z to the FuG 16 ZY, which required an aerial mounted beneath the port wing centre section. Mountings for the ETC 501 under-fuselage rack, which was an option on many previous models, had to be shifted 7.9in further forward due to the new

THE FW 190 A-8 WAS THE VERSION BUILT IN THE GREATEST NUMBERS AND IS WIDELY REGARDED AS THE 'DEFINITIVE' 190.

FOCKE-WULF FW 190

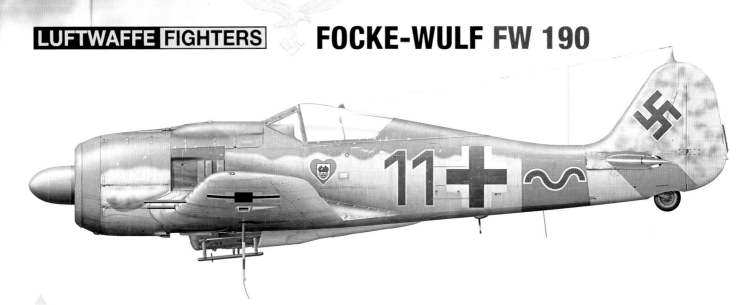

Fw 190 A-8

'Red 11' of 14./ JG 54 at Mörtitz in Germany, November 1944.

fuselage fuel tank. In addition, mountings for WGr 21 rocket tubes were built as standard. Later examples of the A-8 were fitted with a bulged cockpit canopy which significantly improved visibility.

As one of Germany's two most important front line fighters, alongside the Bf 109, at a time when Albert Speer was radically reorganising aircraft production on a national scale, the Fw 190 A-8 was built in huge quantities at numerous dispersed sites. Focke-Wulf itself made at least 1579, from the first examples in March 1944 to the end of the war. Other companies involved in manufacturing the A-8 were WFG, Heinkel, Weserflug, Fieseler, Arado, Concordia, LBB, AGO and Norddeutsche Dornier. It is believed that a total of some 5100 were made but production figures are sketchy or entirely lacking for

the period from December 1944 to April 1945.

Production of the Fw 190 A-9 began in mid-1944 with the introduction of the new BMW 801 S (TS) engine. It had the same capacity as the D-2 at 41.8 litres but produced 2000hp at 2700rpm at sea level, compared to just 1700hp in the same conditions for the D-2. To go with the BMW 801 S (TS) a more efficient radiator was fitted, along with a more heavily armoured oil tank. As a result the cowling was lengthened by 30mm. The first production A-9 was built by Focke-Wulf at Cottbus in August 1944. Norddeutsche Dornier joined in during October and Heinkel started to produce it during November. AGO and Arado also began to build the A-9 from January 1945. Details of exactly how many A-9s were built are scant but estimates range from 500 to 1000.

FW 190 D-9, D-11 AND D-13

The Fw 190 B and C were attempts to build a high-altitude version of the type. The 'B' was to be based on the A-3 but with wings lengthened to 40ft 8¼in. It was to have a pressure cabin and a GM-1 boost for its BMW 801 D-2 engine. The 'C' was an attempt to build a Fw 190 fitted with a turbosupercharged powerplant, either a DB 603 or Jumo 213, plus the longer wings and pressure cabin originally planned for the Fw 190 B. A larger tailfin was designed for it too.

By the beginning of 1943, Focke-Wulf's design team had prepared plans for an advanced and entirely new fighter that would replace the Fw 190 A series completely. These were submitted to the RLM in April 1943 and received the designation Ta 153 – the 'Ta' replacing 'Fw' in honour of the company's now-chief executive

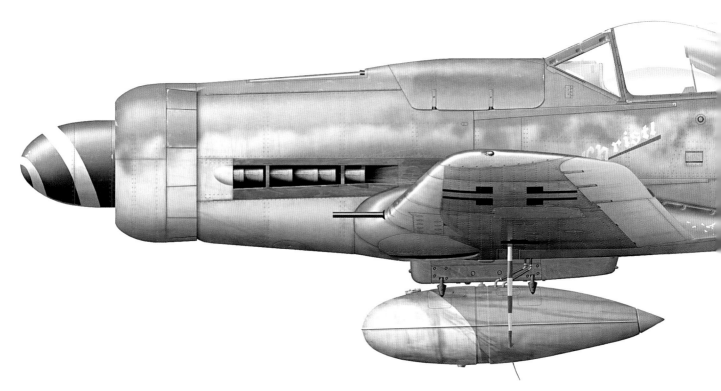

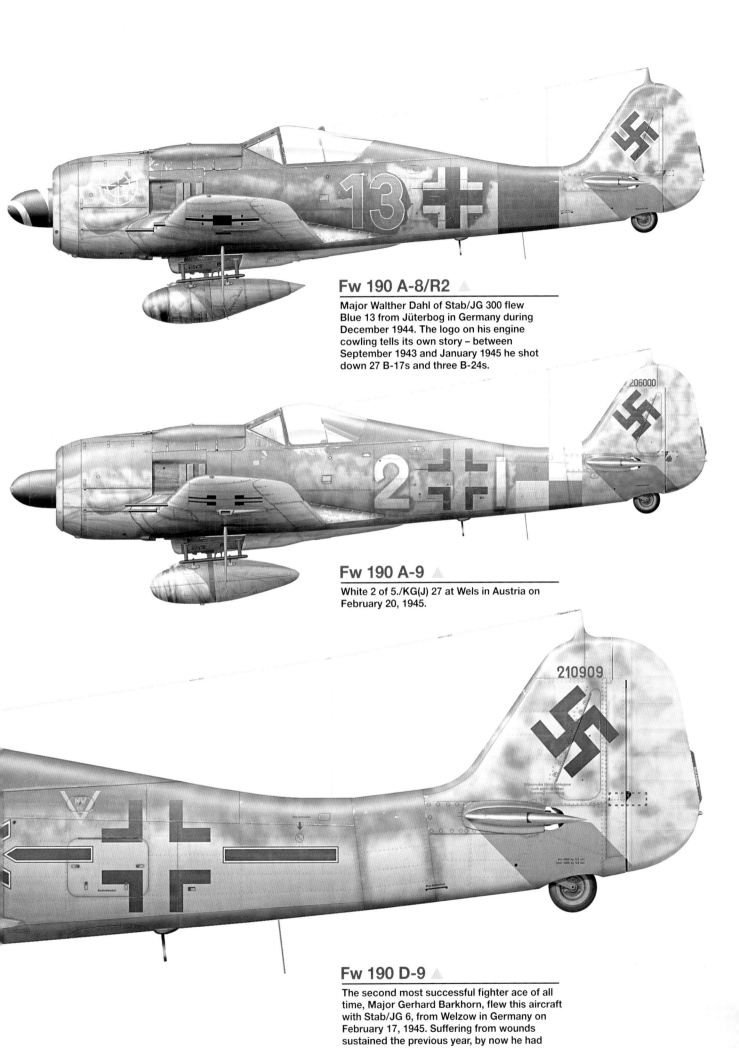

Fw 190 A-8/R2 ▲

Major Walther Dahl of Stab/JG 300 flew
Blue 13 from Jüterbog in Germany during
December 1944. The logo on his engine
cowling tells its own story – between
September 1943 and January 1945 he shot
down 27 B-17s and three B-24s.

Fw 190 A-9 ▲

White 2 of 5./KG(J) 27 at Wels in Austria on
February 20, 1945.

Fw 190 D-9 ▲

The second most successful fighter ace of all
time, Major Gerhard Barkhorn, flew this
aircraft with Stab/JG 6, from Welzow in Germany on
February 17, 1945. Suffering from wounds
sustained the previous year, by now he had
already scored his 301st and final victory.

FOCKE-WULF FW 190

Kurt Tank. Within a short time, however, the Ta 153 was rejected on the grounds that it would cause too much disruption to established production lines at a time when new fighters were desperately needed on every front.

Therefore, on August 17, 1943, Focke-Wulf submitted a version of the design that used as many existing parts as possible – the Ta 152. This too was eventually rejected, for the same reasons. Kurt Tank tried again during a meeting on January 13-14, 1944, and stressed that the standard Ta 152 A would be produced alongside a high-altitude version, the Ta 152 H, from the outset.

In addition, he proposed an interim solution to the problem of improving the Fw 190. By now, issues with the 1750hp inverted V12 Jumo 213 engine had largely been resolved – what if it could be fitted to the latest existing Fw 190 airframe, the A-8, with a minimal number of additional changes to accommodate it?

The RLM, while remaining unconvinced about the Ta 152, reluctantly approved Tank's interim solution and work on the Fw 190 D began. Earlier proposals to try the Jumo 213 in the Fw 190 airframe had been allocated the letter 'D' as Fw 190 D-1 and Fw 190 D-2, the difference being that the latter had a pressurised cockpit while the former did not.

As time wore on and the Fw 190 A-8 entered service, plans for the A-9 were already being advanced.

Therefore, it was decided to skip over D-3 to D-8 and, since the new aircraft was being developed alongside the A-9, designate it the D-9.

While the central idea of the D-9 was to retain as many A-9 components as possible, some changes were unavoidable to cope with the sheer size and particularly the length of the Jumo 213 A-1. Avoiding unfavourable changes in the centre of gravity meant the aircraft's tail had to be elongated with a straight 0.5m section being added to the fuselage ahead of the fin.

In addition, the larger fin designed for the Fw 190 C was used. The weight of the engine meant some extra strengthening was needed for the fuselage

around the engine mounts ahead of the cockpit and bigger wheels were added to the undercarriage too.

In many other respects – control linkages, undercarriage legs and electrics, radio equipment and wings – the D-9 was almost identical to its BMW-engined siblings the A-8 and A-9.

The first D-9 prototype was a modified version of the Fw 190 V17 machine, redesignated V17/U1. This had previously been earmarked for the Jumo 213 but fitted with the DB 603 for testing instead. Now this was stripped out and the Jumo type finally installed between late April and early May 1944.

It was flown for the first time on May 17 and just three months later,

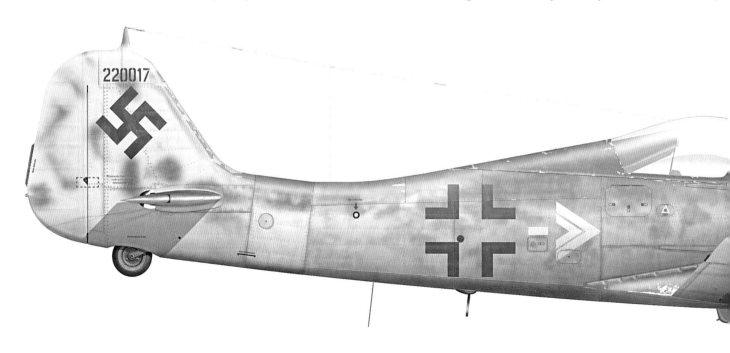

Fw 190 F-8

Black 11 of 5./SG 77 at Cottbus in Germany, early March 1945. Flugplatz Cottbus, a Focke-Wulf factory airfield, became a front-line base in January 1945 as Soviet forces approached. It finally fell to the Russians on April 23, 1945.

in late August, the first production Fw 190 D-9, WNr. 210001, was completed at another Focke-Wulf facility, Sorau in Silesia, in late August. It was armed with just two MG 151s, in the wing roots, and the two MG 131s over the nose. Problems with the aircraft's Jumo 213 A-1 engine, however, prevented further production until mid-September when the second official D-9, WNr. 210002, was

finished. Slowly, bulk production also began at Focke-Wulf's large Cottbus factory. The following month, two subcontractors also began series production – Arbeitgemeinschaft Roland (WFG) at Nordenham and Fieseler at Kassel. Junkers and Siebel also produced large component parts for the type.

It is unknown precisely how many D-9s were built, since

records are incomplete, but at least 670 are documented and it is likely that more than twice that number were ultimately produced since there are no records for December 1944 nor the period from February 1945 to the end of the war.

A handful of Fw 190 D-11s, at least 17, were also built. The D-11 was fitted with the improved Jumo 213 F engine, had an enlarged

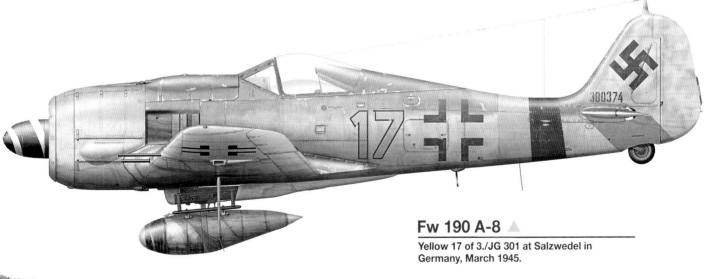

Fw 190 A-8

Yellow 17 of 3./JG 301 at Salzwedel in Germany, March 1945.

Fw 190 D-11

Leutnant Otto Leisner flew Double Chevron with VFS (Verbandsführrerschule) des G. d. J. from Bad Wörishofen, Germany, on March 14, 1945. VFS was a training school for unit leaders established by Adolf Galland in September 1945.

FOCKE-WULF FW 190

supercharger air intake on the starboard side cowling and a larger diameter wooden propeller. Armament consisted of two MK 108s in the outer wing positions and two MG 151s in the inboard wing positions. The engine cowling MG 131s were deleted and a smooth streamlined plate was fitted instead.

Finally, the D-13 also briefly entered production. Every example built was a D-13/R11, which meant each was fitted with equipment for bad weather flying – including PKS12 and K-23 steering and autopilot systems, a heated windscreen, the FuG 125 radio and hydraulic boost for its ailerons.

FW 190 F AND G

Like the Fw 190 B and C, the Fw 190 E never entered production. In November 1942 it was proposed that a dedicated reconnaissance version of the Fw 190 should be built, the E-1, but it was eventually decided that this was unnecessary. What was required, however, was a version of the aircraft that featured built-in attachment points for ground-attack weaponry but which remained capable of operating in the fighter role depending on the circumstances. Various versions of the Bf 109 had been equipped for ground-attack but the type's diminutive size made it ill-suited to carrying substantial payloads. The

Fw 190, on the other hand, could become a capable fighter-bomber with only minor modifications.

The first attempt to create a dedicated Schlachtflugzeug (ground-attack aircraft) had been the Fw 190 A-3/U3, devised in May 1942. This had extra armour plates fitted around and beneath the engine, on the sides of the fuselage and on the undercarriage doors. A variety of different armament options were proposed, ranging from bombs to under-wing cannon pods. Just 12 examples were constructed. Next came the A-4/U3, featuring the same armour and weapon options as its predecessor. In addition, the A-3/

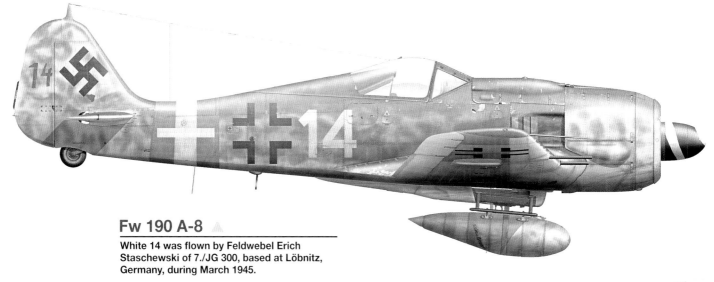

Fw 190 A-8

White 14 was flown by Feldwebel Erich Staschewski of 7./JG 300, based at Löbnitz, Germany, during March 1945.

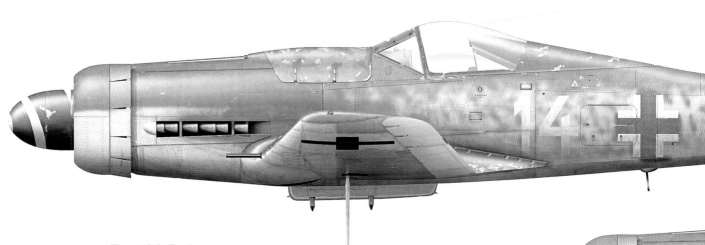

Fw 190 D-9

White 14 of 9./JG 2 at Ettinghausen in Germany, March 1945.

Fw 190 D-9

Oberleutnant Hans Dortenmann of 14./JG 26 flew Black 1 while based at Varrelbusch, Germany, in March 1945. Eighteen of Dortenmann's 38 victories were won while flying this D-9 – making him the most successful pilot with this type.

U3's centreline ETC 501 bomb rack featured the ER-4 adapter, which allowed the Fw 190A-4/U3 to carry a set of four SC50 bombs. Again, only a handful, perhaps a dozen, are believed to have been made.

Next came another small-run type, the A-5/U3. This had two ETC 50 racks under each wing and a hefty total armour weight of 794lb. The A-5/U3 was scheduled for limited production in December 1942 with the ultimate goal of using it as the pattern aircraft for the full production Fw 190 F ground-attack aircraft, scheduled to enter production in June 1943.

Everything proceeded according

to plan until April 1943, when Focke-Wulf changed its mind. The A-4/U3 became officially known as the Fw 190 F-1, while the remaining A-5/U3s became Fw 190 F-2s. A total of up to 270 are believed to have been produced.

The template for true mass production of the Friedrich became, instead, the A-5/U17 which was built as the F-3. This was similar to the A-5/U3 but had its outer wing gun positions deleted. Armament was fixed at a pair of MG 17s on the nose and MG 151 20mm cannon in the wing roots. It also had a FuG 16 ZS radio which used army frequencies, allowing the pilot to

communicate effectively with the forces on the ground that he was supporting.

Most F-3s left the factory – they were all built by Arado – with a modification pack already fitted. The Fw 190 F-3/R1 had an ETC 501 bomb rack with ER 4 adapter under its fuselage plus two ETC 50s under each wing it could carry up to eight SC50 50kg bombs. These could be dropped all at once or in pairs using a control device fitted to the aircraft's cockpit known as the kleine Abwurfelektrik (small electrical release). The extra weight of the bombs caused the aircraft to become unwieldy and

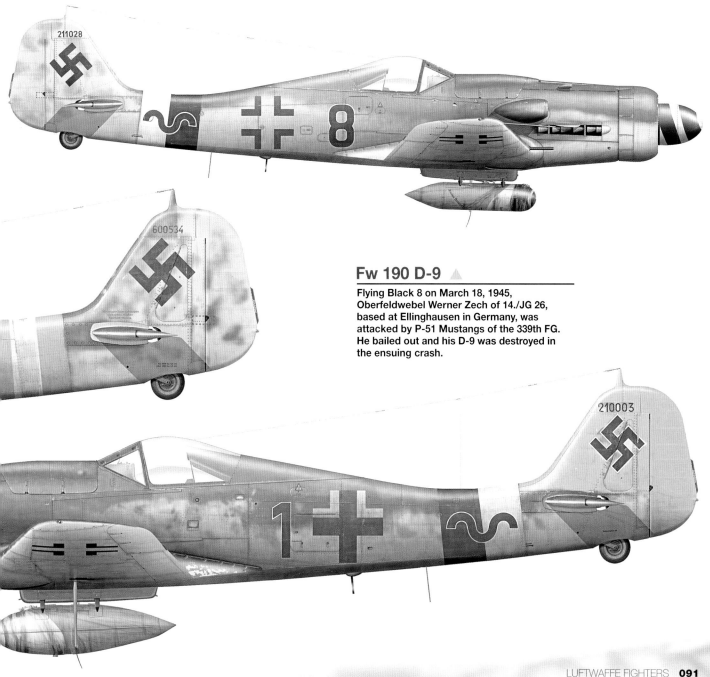

Fw 190 D-9 ▲

Flying Black 8 on March 18, 1945, Oberfeldwebel Werner Zech of 14./JG 26, based at Ellinghausen in Germany, was attacked by P-51 Mustangs of the 339th FG. He bailed out and his D-9 was destroyed in the ensuing crash.

FOCKE-WULF FW 190

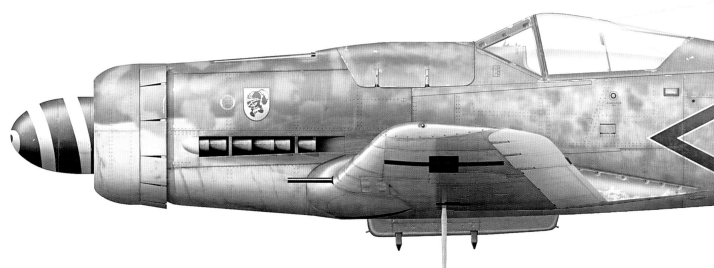

top speed dropped dramatically to just 326mph. Therefore most had their nose-mounted machine guns removed for bombing missions.

Most of the 432 F-3s produced were built between April and December 1943. Production then dropped to a trickle but continued until the last five were built during March 1944. The first units to receive them were I./SKG 10 in France, I./SG 1 and II./SG 1 in Russia and II./SG 2 in Sicily.

The F-4 was essentially an F-3 with a refined release system, allowing bombs to be dropped one at a time. However, with the Fw 190 A-8 now in prospect the A-5 airframe on which the F-4 was to be based was becoming increasingly outdated.

Therefore, the F-4 was cancelled before it could enter even the prototype stage and a revised version was designed based on the A-8, to be known as the F-8. This had the same armament as the A-8 but without the outer wing positions. The F-8 also differed from the A-8 in having a modified injector on its compressor which gave enhanced performance during low level flying for several minutes.

F-8 production was almost on a par with that of the A-8 – an incredible 3614 being built, 2264 of them by Arado and 1350 by Norddeutsche Dornier. A new development based on the A-9, the F-9, was introduced in January 1945 with some 400 built, though exact figures are unknown. Yet more advanced versions were planned but none were produced.

During the autumn of 1942, a long-range version of the Fw 190 F was proposed – the Fw 190 G. This had a centreline ETC 501 bomb rack but also had all

armament removed except for the MG 151 cannon in the wing roots. The deletion of any nose mounted weapons allowed for the installation of an additional oil tank to improve the endurance of the aircraft's BMW 801 D-2 engine.

A critical factor in the Fw 190 G's design was the ability to carry a drop tank under each wing and since Focke-Wulf did not have the appropriate racks to enable this, it bought in faired racks from Weserflug that had been designed for use on the Ju 87 Stuka – known as the VTr. Ju 87.

While they certainly did the job, these racks reduced the aircraft's speed to an appalling 298mph. Two prototype Fw 190 G-1s, based on the Fw 190 A-4, were flown in late 1942 and early 1943 but the type did not enter production. However, a small number of a version based on the A-5, the Fw 190 G-2, did. This was followed by the G-3, which had fittings made in-house by Focke-Wulf. Some 550 of these were made – all by Focke-Wulf itself. With the advent of the standard Fw 190 A-8, the G-series jumped to the G-8 and a further 700 or so were built.

TA 152

Two standard fighter versions with different engines were proposed by Focke-Wulf for its Fw 190 replacement: the Ta 152 A and the Ta 152 B. The former was to have a Jumo 213 A and the latter a Jumo 213 E, with the Daimler-Benz DB 603 G as a backup for either.

It was intended that the finished fighter, whatever its engine, would be able to function as either a fighter or fighter-bomber. Standard armament was to be a single

MK 103 or MK 108 firing through the nose and MG 151s in both the wing roots and outer wing positions, for a total of five guns.

The Ta 152 A/B took the basic A-8 airframe and lengthened the forward fuselage by 0.772m to accommodate either new engine and an engine mounted MK 108 cannon. This fuselage extension

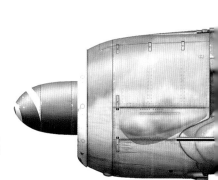

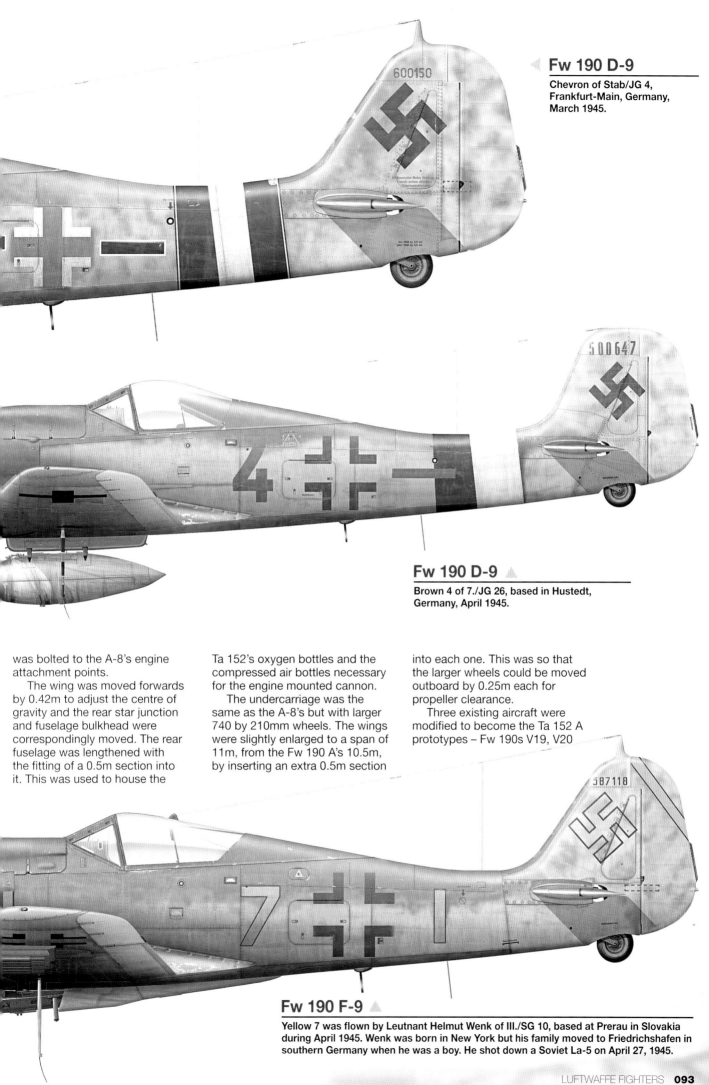

Fw 190 D-9

Chevron of Stab/JG 4,
Frankfurt-Main, Germany,
March 1945.

Fw 190 D-9

Brown 4 of 7./JG 26, based in Hustedt,
Germany, April 1945.

was bolted to the A-8's engine attachment points.

The wing was moved forwards by 0.42m to adjust the centre of gravity and the rear star junction and fuselage bulkhead were correspondingly moved. The rear fuselage was lengthened with the fitting of a 0.5m section into it. This was used to house the

Ta 152's oxygen bottles and the compressed air bottles necessary for the engine mounted cannon.

The undercarriage was the same as the A-8's but with larger 740 by 210mm wheels. The wings were slightly enlarged to a span of 11m, from the Fw 190 A's 10.5m, by inserting an extra 0.5m section

into each one. This was so that the larger wheels could be moved outboard by 0.25m each for propeller clearance.

Three existing aircraft were modified to become the Ta 152 A prototypes – Fw 190s V19, V20

Fw 190 F-9

Yellow 7 was flown by Leutnant Helmut Wenk of III./SG 10, based at Prerau in Slovakia during April 1945. Wenk was born in New York but his family moved to Friedrichshafen in southern Germany when he was a boy. He shot down a Soviet La-5 on April 27, 1945.

FOCKE-WULF FW 190

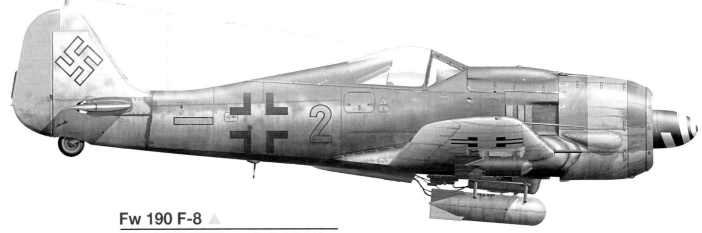

Fw 190 F-8 ▲

Yellow 2, WNr. 586875, served with 6./SG 10
at Hörsching, Austria, during late April 1945.

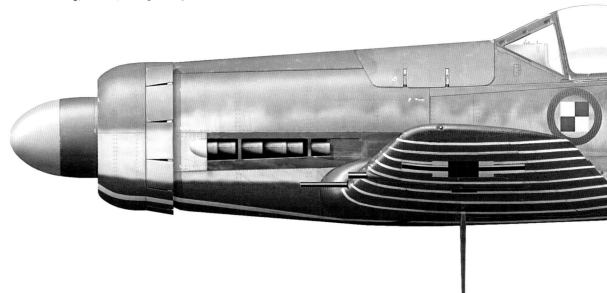

and V21. There were no Ta 152 B prototypes since the Jumo 213 E engine had been seriously delayed.

V19 first flew with its Jumo 213 A on July 7, 1943. It had a new tail, later to be seen on the Fw 190 D-9, and a 50cm fuselage extension but no armament. Its initial task was to investigate engine performance and handling.

Focke-Wulf applied for permission to give the Ta 152 A development priority on October 8, 1943, but this was denied. The second prototype, Fw 190 V20 TI+IG, made its first flight on November 23, 1943, with a Jumo 213 CV engine. This unarmed airframe was used for engine checks, speed trials, fuel system and hydraulic tests.

Tank had been considering a high-altitude version of the Ta 152 to compete with the Bf 109 H and shortly after he submitted plans for the Ta 152 H to the RLM, on December 7, 1943, the ministry ordered six prototypes. It stipulated, however, that these should be built from standard A-8 airframes with the minimum

possible number of changes.

The Ta 152 H had the same A-8 airframe alternations as the 152 A but the fuselage centre section was designed as a pressurized chamber with a volume of about one cubic metre, sealed with DHK 880 paste. The sliding cockpit canopy was sealed with a tube partly filled with foam rubber.

When the pilot activated it, a one litre compressed air bottle pumped up the tube. In order to get out of the aircraft, the tube had to be emptied first – which meant it would be difficult for the pilot to escape in an emergency. In addition, wingspan was increased to 14.4m (47ft 3in) from the standard Fw 190 A's 10.5m (34ft 5in). On December 20, 1943, Tank resubmitted his request for the Ta 152 A to be given development priority but this was again denied. Tank's efforts to persuade the RLM of the aircraft's merits resulted, at the meeting on January 13-14, 1944, in the Fw 190 D-9 being approved as an interim measure.

The first Ta 152 A test airframe, V19, crashed on February 16, 1944,

when the right undercarriage leg locking bolt failed but the damage was repaired and testing was resumed. By now, the Jumo 213 E engine planned for the Ta 152 B had been subject to serious delays so another powerplant, the Daimler-Benz DB 603 L, was identified for the aircraft under the designation Ta 152 C. Like the A and B, this was proposed

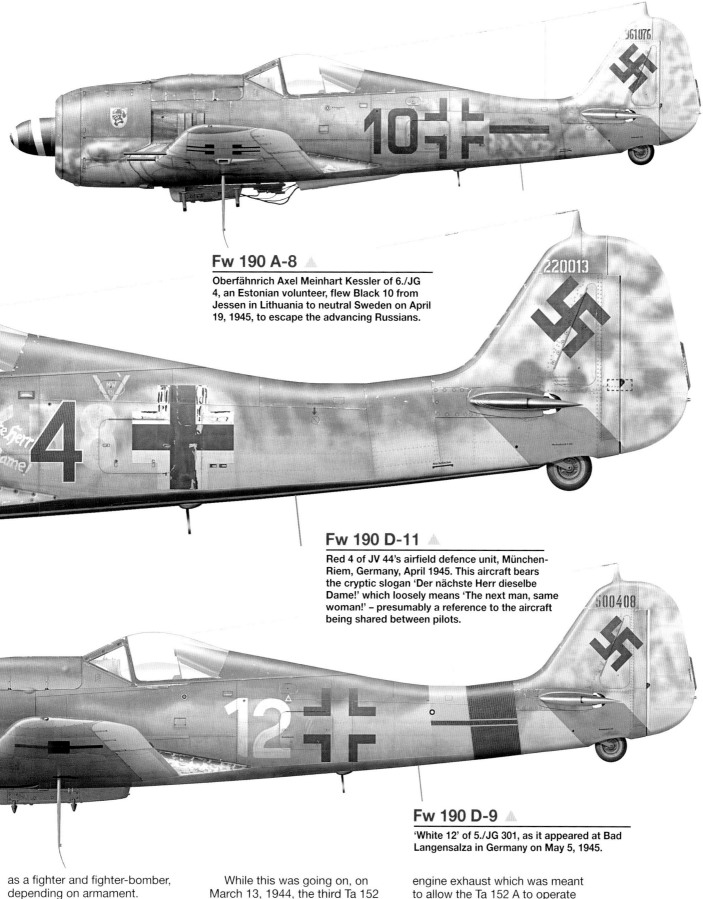

Fw 190 A-8

Oberfähnrich Axel Meinhart Kessler of 6./JG 4, an Estonian volunteer, flew Black 10 from Jessen in Lithuania to neutral Sweden on April 19, 1945, to escape the advancing Russians.

Fw 190 D-11

Red 4 of JV 44's airfield defence unit, München-Riem, Germany, April 1945. This aircraft bears the cryptic slogan 'Der nächste Herr dieselbe Dame!' which loosely means 'The next man, same woman!' – presumably a reference to the aircraft being shared between pilots.

Fw 190 D-9

'White 12' of 5./JG 301, as it appeared at Bad Langensalza in Germany on May 5, 1945.

as a fighter and fighter-bomber, depending on armament.

The Ta 152 C had the same fuselage extensions and larger wheels as the other members of the 152 family and the same wings as the Ta 152 A/B but without outer wing gun positions. Instead, provision was made to carry a pair of MG 151/20 machine guns in the upper cowling above the engine.

While this was going on, on March 13, 1944, the third Ta 152 A prototype, Fw 190 V21 TI+IH, made its first flight with a Jumo 213 CV. It had the 50cm fuselage extension, another new tail type, the now familiar Ta 152 tail, no armament and gun port openings in its engine cowling. It was used to test, along with V20, a glare-reducing flame damper over the

engine exhaust which was meant to allow the Ta 152 A to operate as a night fighter without special modifications.

The damper, however, imposed such a severe performance penalty on the aircraft's engine that it was abandoned on April 18, 1944. Less than a month later V21 managed a top speed of 335mph at sea level and on May 5, 1944, it was

FOCKE-WULF FW 190

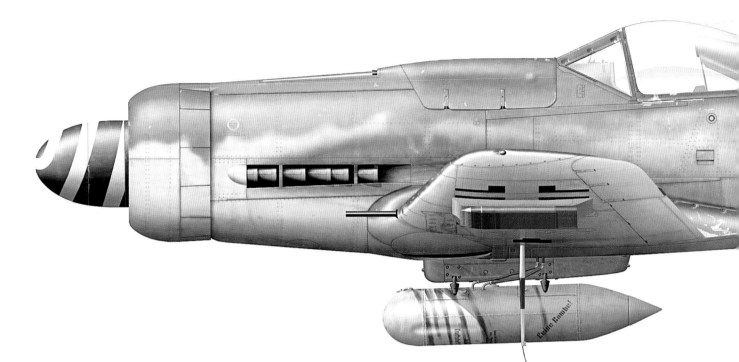

transferred to Rechlin for further trials. The Ta 152 A was now ready for full production – and was promptly cancelled by the RLM in July 1944. The Ta 152 B standard fighter design was left in limbo as its Jumo 213 E engine was still delayed and the 152 H, using the same engine, was given higher priority.

This resulted in the odd situation where, because the Ta 152 A was cancelled and the Ta 152 B was stalled, the Ta 152 C became the focus of efforts to create a 'standard' Ta 152 fighter.

Its development, however, had only just begun and was therefore behind that of the specialised Ta 152 H which had been worked on since December 1943.

The first airframe intended to test components and handling for the planned Ta 152 H took place on July 13, 1944. But just 36 minutes after take-off for a ferrying flight, Fw 190 V33/U1, GH+KW, crash-landed and suffered severe damage.

This was a major setback for the Ta 152 H. The Ta 152 C programme also suffered a big

setback when one of its first prototypes, former Ta 152 A tester Fw 190 V20, being converted into V20/U1, was destroyed in an air raid on August 5, 1944.

Fortunately, the RLM had ordered six prototypes of the Ta 152 H and work on the second one was nearly complete. Fw 190 V30/U1 GH+KT was able to make its first flight the day after the air raid and testing with its early Jumo 213 E engine commenced.

V30/U1 was transferred to the Rechlin test centre on August 19 but during another high altitude

Fw 190 F-9

Chevron/Black 1, possibly of Stab/SG 10, at Budweis in Czechoslovakia, May 1945.

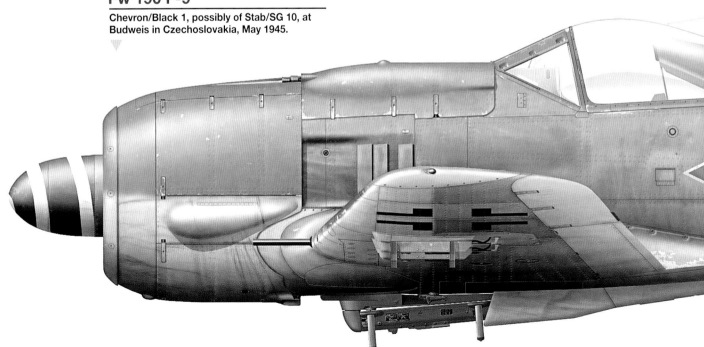

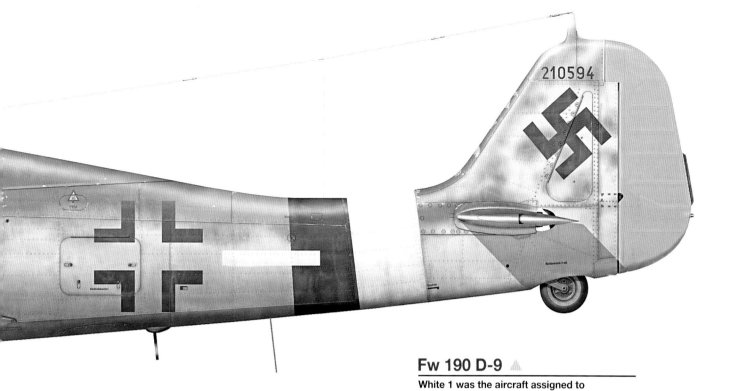

Fw 190 D-9 ▲

White 1 was the aircraft assigned to Oberleutnant Peter Crump of 5./JG 26 at Husum, Germany, May 5, 1945. However Crump, who had originally joined the Luftwaffe in 1937, had flown his last combat mission three days earlier.

flight with Flugkapitän Alfred Thomas at the controls, the Jumo 213 E caught fire. The aircraft crashed and Thomas was killed.

The third Ta 152 H prototype, Fw 190 V29/U1 GH+KS, first flew on September 24, 1944, and was sent to Rechlin three days later to get the testing process quickly under way. Rechlin's pilots concluded that the aircraft required trim changes, had 'uncomfortable' stall behaviour and suffered poor stability in the vertical axis but was otherwise stable.

November 3 saw the first Ta 152 C test aircraft finally taking to the skies – Fw 190 V21/U1, formerly used as part of the Ta 152 A programme. With the planned DB 603 L engine delayed, it was powered by a stopgap DB 603 E instead. On November 18 it was handed over to Daimler-Benz itself for conversion to the new DB 603 LA engine.

Fw 190 V18 became the fourth Ta 152 H test aircraft as V18/U2, starting with a first

flight in its new configuration on November 19, 1944. Meanwhile, now that the Jumo 213 E was finally proving more reliable, the Ta 152 B was revived. Since the Daimler-Benz powered Ta 152 C already occupied the standard fighter role, it was envisioned that the 152 B could become a Zerstörer (heavy fighter) to fill the role vacated by the

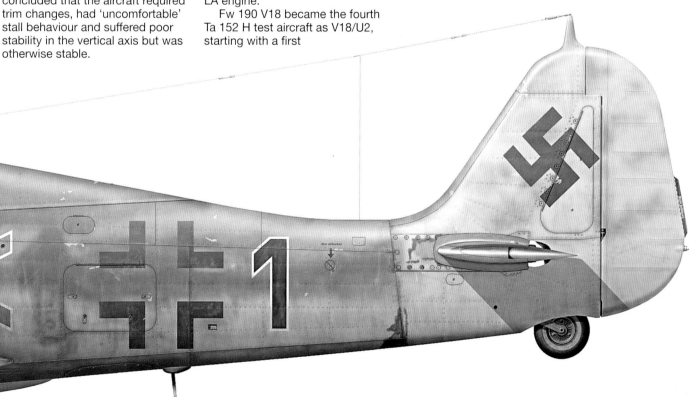

FOCKE-WULF FW 190

recently cancelled Me 410.

The Ta 152 B-5 was intended to be similar to the C but with a Jumo engine and a reduced armament – one MK 103 in the engine and another in each wing root. It was planned that production would begin at Erla in May 1945 and Gotha in July 1945.

The war situation was deteriorating rapidly, but sufficient testing had been done for the Ta 152 H to enter full production in late November 1944, just 11 months after the first prototypes had been ordered.

Neuhausen, near Cottbus in Brandenburg, was chosen as the Ta 152 production centre and work began slowly. While the facilities were available for mass production, the materials and components were not. There were continuous delays at the factory as missing parts were tracked down for the first run of Ta 152 H-0 aircraft.

Focke-Wulf chief test pilot Hans Sander flew the first machine off the production line, WNr. 150 001 CW+CA, on November 24, 1944. He later recalled: "I had to put the first production machine down on its belly away from Cottbus because while climbing out after takeoff the engine suddenly stopped receiving fuel. A hydraulic valve had somehow been installed in the fuel line. I

received a bottle of schnapps, hard to come by in those days, as compensation. Everything was okay with the second machine."

The second machine was first flown on November 29 and the third on December 3. A total of 21 H-0s had been completed by the end of December. These had no wing fuel tanks or MW 50/GM 1 boost. Production was in full swing during early January but on January 16, a group of 40 USAAF Lightnings and Mustangs attacked the airfield at Neuhausen, where the new Ta 152s had been gathered prior to delivery to III./JG 301, the first unit intended to operate them. Fourteen brand new 152s were completely destroyed and another was damaged.

In the meantime, the Ta 152 C programme was still forging ahead. Three more prototypes had been constructed, this time from scratch – Ta 152 V6 VH+EY, V7 CI+XM and

V8 GW+QA – flying on December 12, January 8 and January 15 respectively.

Plans were now on the drawing board too for further variants – a Focke-Wulf production schedule dating from January 1945 indicates plans for a two-seater Ta 152 S-1 based on the Ta 152 C-1, to be built

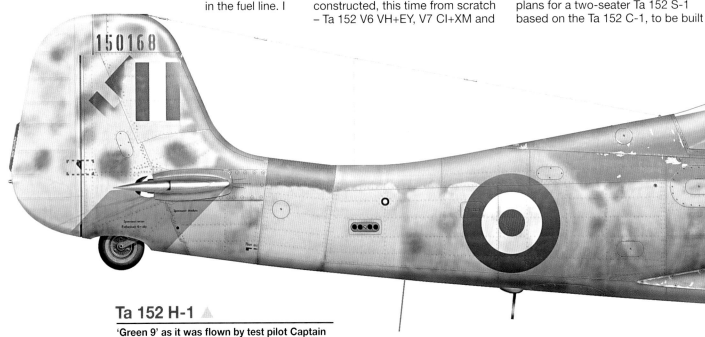

Ta 152 H-1

'Green 9' as it was flown by test pilot Captain Eric 'Winkle' Brown as part of the Enemy Aircraft Flight at Farnborough, England, on October 22, 1945. The aircraft is believed to have previously been piloted by Obfw. Willi Reschke of JG 301 in combat during April 1945.

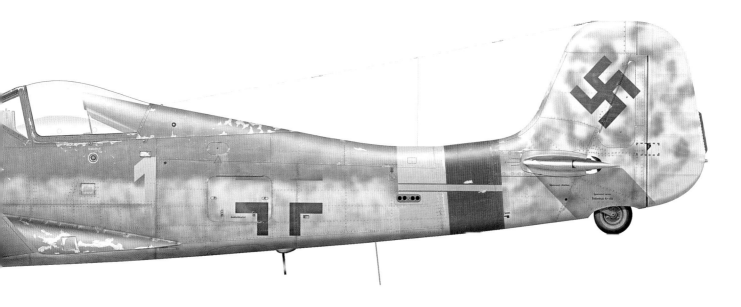

Ta 152 H-0 ⚠

Yellow 1 of 11./JG 301, at Alteno in Germany, January 1945.

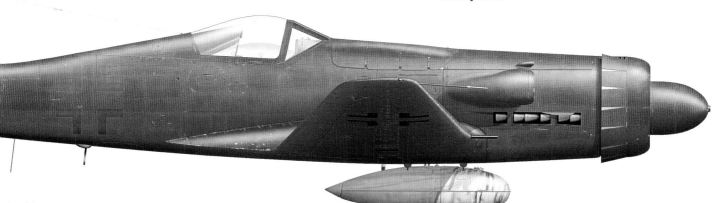

by Blohm & Voss from April 1945, the reconnaissance version Ta 152 E-1 with RB 75/30 camera in its fuselage, and Ta 152 C-11 torpedo launching aircraft.

Another 20 Ta 152s, H-0s and H-1s, would be completed in January and three more in February before production ceased, giving a total of 43 production machines, plus 11 prototype/experimental airframes. ●

Ta 152 H-1 ⚠

Ahead of a meeting at Rechlin to discuss the Ta 152 on March 22, 1945, Oberstleutnant Fritz Aufhammer of Stab/JG 301 ordered that his Ta 152 H-1 be painted bright red so German flak gunners would not shooting it down.

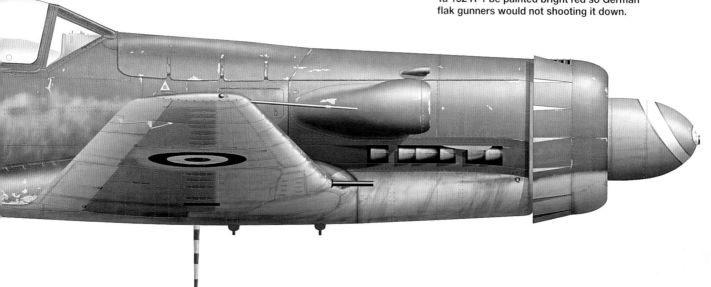

JUNKERS JU 88

JUNKERS

The versatile Junkers Ju 88 was the Luftwaffe's newest aircraft at the outbreak of the Second World War. Designed as a fast bomber, it proved well suited to night fighter duties when required and Junkers put a great deal of time and effort into continually improving its capabilities as the war went on.

1936-1945

hen the 1934 Kampfzerstörer requirement was split in two and the Bf 110 became the Luftwaffe's new zerstörer unopposed, the other half of the requirement necessitated a new design competition. The split was made in mid-1935 and a new schnellbomber or 'fast bomber' requirement was sent out to four companies – Messerschmitt, Focke-Wulf, Henschel and Junkers.

The Focke-Wulf entry was eliminated early on but the other three firms were given contracts to construct prototypes. Messerschmitt's entry, the Bf 162, was a version of the Bf 110; Henschel made the Hs 127 and Junkers presented the Ju 88. While the Messerschmitt design was attractive, particularly because it would share so many

components with the Bf 110 and therefore keep costs down, it was inflexible and lacked the multirole capability inherent in the larger Junkers design.

By the time the Hs 127 V1 was ready for its first flight, in September 1937, a decision had already been made to proceed with the Ju 88 as the Luftwaffe's new fast bomber. Over the next two years the design evolved rapidly – the pre-production prototype V6 apparently sharing only 35% of its components with the V4.

One of the last two prototypes constructed, the V7, was used to test a solid unglazed nose and fixed forward-firing guns for a projected fighter version. It first flew on September 27, 1938.

It was not until February 1940 that the first fighter version of the

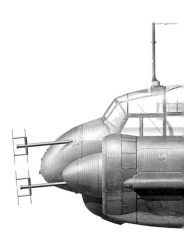

JU 88 C-4

The most successful night fighter ace of the Second World War at the time of his death with 12 victories, Leutnant Hans Hahn of 3./NJG 2 flew R4+NL from his unit's base at Gilzen-Rijen in Holland during September 1941. The following month, on October 11, he was attacking an RAF Airspeed Oxford twin-engine trainer close to Grantham in Lincolnshire when he accidentally collided with it and crashed. Both his flight engineer Unteroffizier Helmut Scheidt and wireless operator Unteroffizier Ernst-Wilhelm Meissler were also killed.

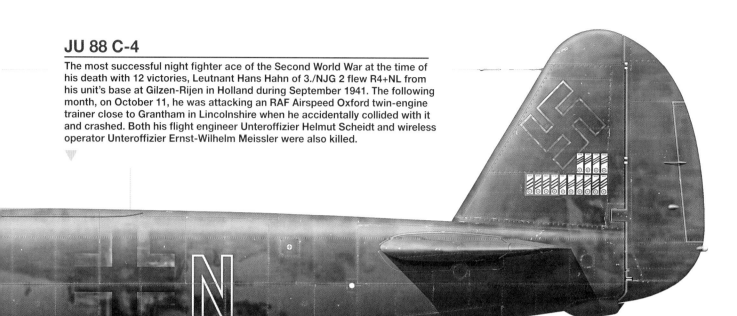

JU 88

JU 88 C-4

Leutnant Heinz Rökker of 1./NJG 2, based at Kaselli on Crete, flew R4+IL during May 1942 – before he had achieved a single combat victory. He would go on to become one of the Luftwaffe's most successful night fighter aces with 64 victories between June 1942 and March 15, 1945. When this publication was written, during October 2016, Rökker was the only pilot of any of the aircraft depicted to still be alive, aged 95.

JU 88 C-6

R4+FM was flown by Leutnant Wilhelm Beier of 10./NJG 1, based at Leeuwarden, Holland, during October 1942. On the night of the 15/16th of that month he would shoot down an RAF B-24 Liberator at 10.13pm, a Short Stirling at 10.16pm, another at 10.19pm and finally an Avro Manchester at 10.52pm.

JUNKERS JU 88

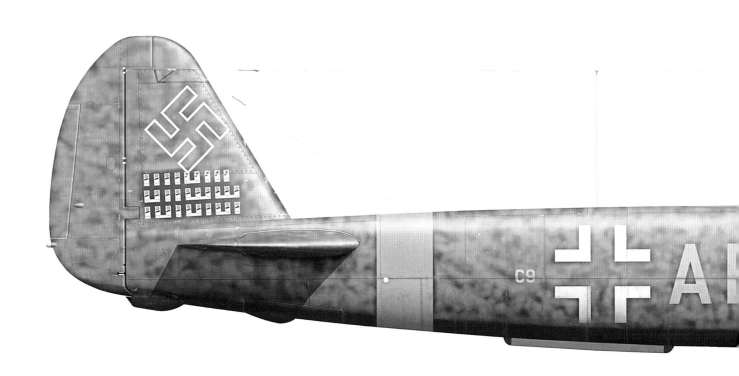

JU 88 C-6

Hauptmann Eduard Schröder of 12./NJG 3 flew D5+GX from Grove in Denmark during December 1943. Schröder achieved 24 night victories with NJG 3 but had previously claimed five day victories with II./JG 53, three of them while serving on the Eastern Front.

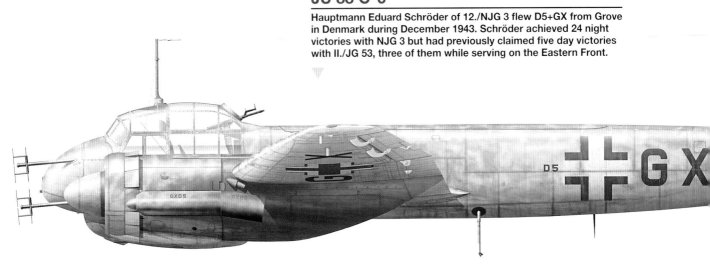

JU 88 C-6

8V+BM of 4./NJG 200, based at Orsha in Belarus, USSR, during the harsh winter conditions of January 1944.

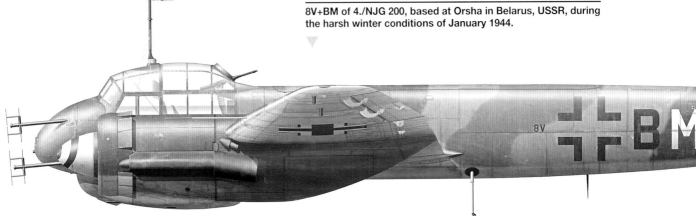

JU 88 C-6

Born into the German aristocracy, Heinrich Prinz zu Sayn Wittgenstein joined the Hitler Youth in 1932 before joining the Luftwaffe in 1937. He was initially an observer/navigator aboard Ju 88 and He 111 bombers before retraining as a pilot during the winter of 1940-41 and transferring to the night fighter force during August 1941. By June 1943, with the rank of hauptmann, he was a member of Stab./IV./NJG 5 based at Insterburg-Prussia in Germany. He had been used to flying a Bf 110 but on the night of June 24, 1943, his usual aircraft was unserviceable so he took up this Ju 88 C-6 instead – C9+AE. He was so impressed with its performance, shooting down four Lancaster bombers that night, that he never flew the Bf 110 again.

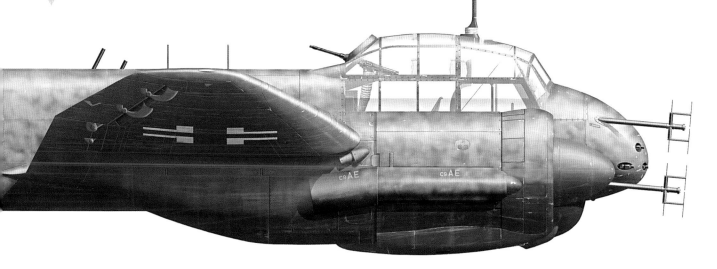

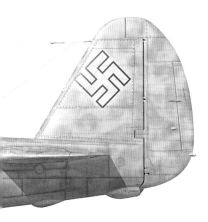

Ju 88, the C-1, began to appear as a factory modification of fully built Ju 88 A-1 airframes rolling off the production lines. Powered by a pair of Jumo 211 engines and armed with three MG 17 machine guns and one MG FF cannon in a solid nose, 20 examples were constructed. Later that year, the same process was used to convert 20 Ju 88 A-5s into the Ju 88 C-2 heavy fighter with the same armament.

A shortage of the BMW 801 engines intended to power it meant that the Ju 88 C-3 heavy fighter was never built but a further 60 A-5s were converted into long-range reconnaissance versions of the C-2, designated the C-4. Both C-2 and C-4 aircraft were used to perform missions over Britain during 1941 by I./NJG 2. The C-5 was intended to be a BMW 801-powered version of the C-4 and suffered the same fate as the C-3.

After the A-1, the next major production model of the Ju 88 was the A-4. Entering service towards the end of 1940, this resolved teething troubles experienced with the A-1. Its revised features included redesigned wingtips, wider fields of fire for defensive weaponry, stronger undercarriage and more powerful engines – either Jumo 211 J-1s or J-2s with wooden-bladed propellers.

Using this upgraded platform as a starting point, Junkers designed the C-6 as both a heavy fighter and night fighter. The standard heavy fighter was equipped with the usual trio of MG 17s and single MG FF/M cannon in its nose but also carried a pair of forward-firing MG FF/Ms in an under-fuselage gondola. For defence it retained a single rearward-firing MG 15 or MG 131.

The night fighter version of the C-6 was a standard production model converted to carry a FuG 202 Lichtenstein BC radar unit or, from the autumn of 1942, a FuG 212 Lichtenstein C-1 radar. Later in the war, some C-6 night fighters were fitted with the FuG 220 Lichtenstein SN-2 plus the C-1, and some of these also had a pair of upwards firing MG 151s installed as a Schräge Musik arrangement. Production of the C-6 as a purpose-built fighter, rather than a conversion like earlier 'C' types, commenced in October 1941 – a year after the A-4 – and all together, some 900 Ju 88 C-6s were manufactured.

During mid-1943 it was decided that since most C-6s were now being converted from heavy fighter to night fighter, production should be switched to a dedicated night fighter, saving time by eliminating the need for post-production alterations. This became the

JUNKERS JU 88

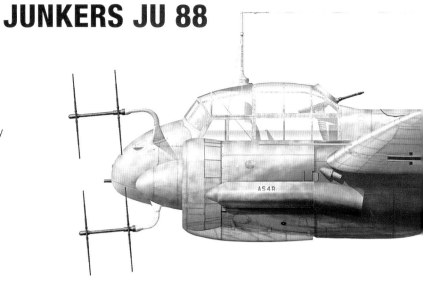

'G' series and the first six pre-production G-0s were constructed by Junkers at Bernburg during December 1943, swiftly followed by 13 full production G-1s that same month. This production line was run in parallel with the introduction of the Ju 188 and Ju 388.

The Ju 88 G-1 was powered by a pair of BMW 801s, since the projected replacement for the now under-powered Jumo 211, the Jumo 213, was not yet available. Its rear fuselage, with a larger re-shaped fin, came from the Ju 188 and all nose armament was deleted. Instead, it carried four forward-firing MG 151 20mm cannon in an under-fuselage pod which was offset to the port side of the fuselage. The radar unit was initially the Lichtenstein BC, although later examples featured the FuG 220 Lichtenstein SN-2. The G-1 was also equipped with the FuG 227 Flensburg passive radar receiver. This device, developed by Siemens and Halske, used wing and tail-mounted dipole

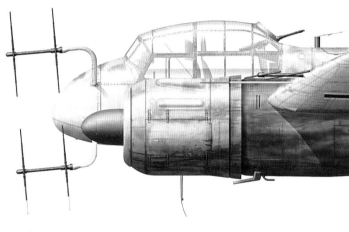

JU 88 C-6

Double chevron C9+AC was flown by Major Hans Leickhardt of the Stab./ II./NJG 5, based at Stubendorf in Germany during December 1944.

JU 88 G-6

9W+EL of 3./NJG 101, depicted as it appeared at Ingolstadt-Manching in Germany during March 1945.

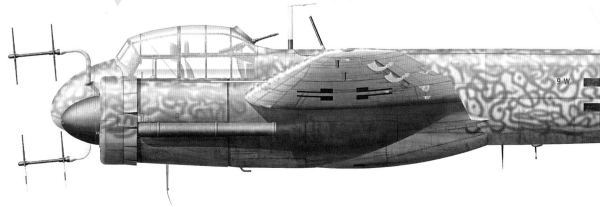

JU 88 C-6

Hauptmann Friedrich Tober flew 4R+AS with 8./NJG 2, based at Gilzen-Rijen, Holland, during March 1944.

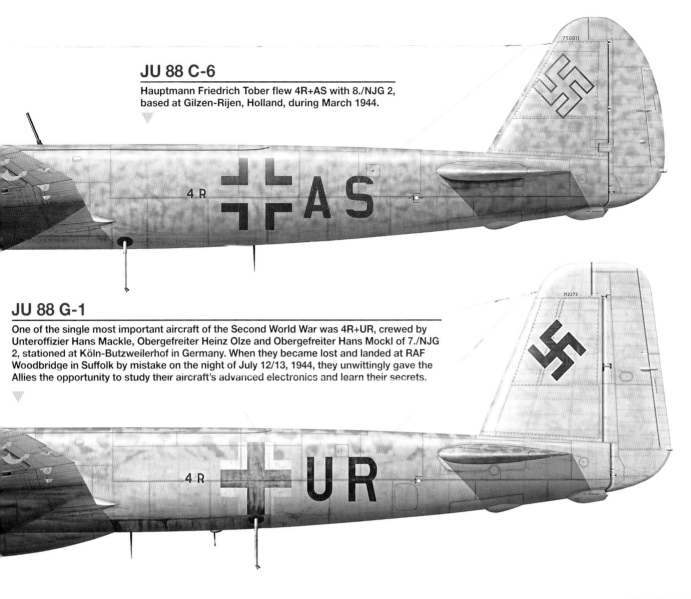

JU 88 G-1

One of the single most important aircraft of the Second World War was 4R+UR, crewed by Unteroffizier Hans Mackle, Obergefreiter Heinz Olze and Obergefreiter Hans Mockl of 7./NJG 2, stationed at Köln-Butzweilerhof in Germany. When they became lost and landed at RAF Woodbridge in Suffolk by mistake on the night of July 12/13, 1944, they unwittingly gave the Allies the opportunity to study their aircraft's advanced electronics and learn their secrets.

antennae and was effectively able to home in one signals from the Monica tail warning radar carried by RAF bombers.

This gave the Luftwaffe's night fighter force a huge advantage by allowing them to track the RAF's aircraft – using their own radar signals against them. However, on July 13, 1944, a Ju 88 G-1 fitted with Flensburg made a wheels-down landing at RAF Woodbridge in Suffolk. The pilot, Hans Mackle, had become completely lost and was nearly out of fuel. Believing he was near Berlin, he put the aircraft down, only to discover his mistake when he and his crew were arrested.

The G-1 was carefully examined by British intelligence who quickly realized the importance of their fortunate discovery and had Monica stripped from all RAF bombers.

Production of the last Ju 88 fighter to see front line service in large numbers, the G-6, began during June 1944. The G-6 differed from the G-1 primarily in being powered by the new Jumo 213 A. It was built in parallel to the G-1 until November 1944, when production switched entirely over to the G-6.

A total of nearly 1200 G-1s and 1050 G-6s were manufactured during 1944, with G-6 production continuing until Junkers' facilities and those of its subcontractors were overrun by the Allies one by one during the spring of 1945.

THE FUG 227 FLENSBURG PASSIVE RADAR RECEIVER GAVE THE LUFTWAFFE'S NIGHT FIGHTER FORCE A HUGE ADVANTAGE.

JUNKERS JU 88

During January 1945, deliveries of another Ju 88 fighter commenced – the long-range night fighter G-10. This featured an extended fuselage to carry more fuel but just 30 were made before the war ended and most if not all of these were converted for use in Mistel flying bomb combinations. Finally, the G-7 went into production during March 1945.

This was broadly similar to the G-6 but with more powerful Jumo 213 E engines installed, necessitating a switch from three-bladed propellers to four-bladed, and was also fitted with pointed-tip longer-span Ju 188 wings. Perhaps fewer than 10 G-7s were built.

The Ju 88 night fighters in all their various forms were generally well liked by their crews and the later 'G' series models were among the most well-equipped and capable German aircraft still flying at the end of the war – surpassing even the dedicated He 219 night fighter. ●

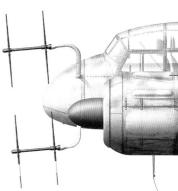

JU 88 G-6

Night fighter ace Hauptmann Herbert Koch 1./NJG 3 flew D5+AH from Grove in Denmark on the night of April 24/25, 1945, and scored the Luftwaffe's 7308th and last night fighter victory of the Second World War. He shot down Halifax bomber JP299 of 58 Squadron Coastal Command west of Skagen at 1.21am on the 25th. The Halifax's 21-year-old pilot Flight Lieutenant Arthur Thomas Charles Wilmot-Dear and his crew were all killed.

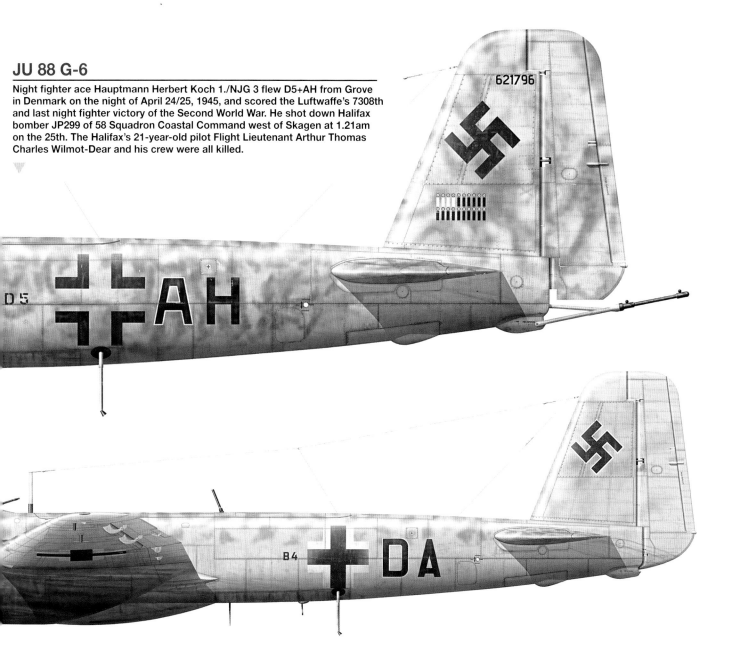

JU 88 G-1

The unfortunate Feldwebel Kurt Gross of 4./NJG 3, based at Kjevik, Norway, was flying B4+DA on April 25, 1945, when he was shot down and killed, along with his two crewmen Reinhard Johnsen and Otto Müller, over Kragerø in Telemark county.

JU 88 G-6

3C+MN of 5./NJG 4 as it appeared at Flensburg, Germany, at the very end of the war – May 1945. The long smooth nose houses the dish of a FuG 240 Berlin N-1 cavity magnetron-based 3 GHz-band centimetric radar system. Only around a dozen examples of this system were built before the war in Europe ended.

DORNIER
DO 17/215/217

Dornier's Do 17 was a bomber and so were its successors – the Do 215 and Do 217. Yet the aircraft's straightforward modern design made it easy to develop. When the Luftwaffe found itself in urgent need of more night fighters, Dornier obliged by adapting its most successful machine to the role.

Production of the 'Flying Pencil' Dornier Do 17 ended in 1940 and the numerous examples still available were withdrawn from front line service when the type's replacement, the Do 217, became available in significant numbers during 1942.

However, with the commencement of the RAF's devastating campaign of night bombing an urgent need arose for more aircraft capable of intercepting them. These aircraft did not need to be particularly manoeuvrable – indeed, they hardly needed to be 'fighters' at all in the conventional sense since no dogfighting or aerobatics would be necessary.

Stable gun platforms were required and with the redundant Do 17 Z available in quantity it made sense to see whether it

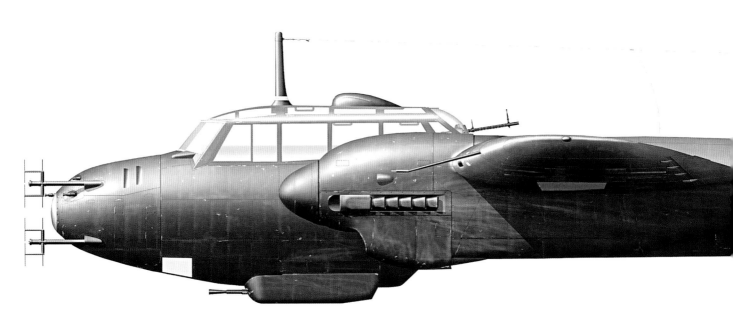

Do 17 Z-7

A stopgap night fighter at best, the Do 17 Z-7 was little more than a cumbersome gun platform. This example is R4+HK of 2./NJG 2, based at Gilzen-Rijen in Holland during October 1941.

could be made to meet that requirement. The result was the Do 17 Z-7 Kauz I. Powered by Bramo 323 P-1 engines, its endurance was increase by fitting an additional fuel tank in the bomb bay. Armour plates were bolted to the solid nose bulkhead to protect the three-strong crew from return fire and it was armed with a trio of MG 17s plus a single MG FF cannon.

A small number of airframes received this modification and further upgrades – including the Spanner-Anlage infrared lamp target-finding system and a heavier armament of four MG 17s and two MG FFs – created the Z-10 Kauz II. Just 10 Kauz IIs were made and one of them was tested with the Lichtenstein radar.

The Do 215 was a made-for-export version of the Do 17 and was largely identical to the Do 17 Z. This meant it too was a candidate for night fighter conversion and a total of 20 B-1s and B-4s were modified to become the Do 215 B-5 or Kauz III. This had the same weaponry as the Kauz II but since the Spanner-Anlage system was ineffective some were subsequently fitted with Lichtenstein 202 radar units during 1942.

As the early Do 17 and 215 night fighters were either destroyed or became obsolete, some thought was given to building new a night fighter based on the Do 217 E design. Fitted with a solid nose crammed with four MG 17s and a pair of MG FFs like its forebears, the Do 217 E became the Do 217 J.

Do 215 B-5

Night fighter ace Oberleutnant Paul Gildner of 5./NJG 2, based at Rijen, Holland, was flying R4+SN on June 2/3, 1942, when he shot down a Short Stirling at 3.10am. The bomber went down 70km west of Petten in North Holland.

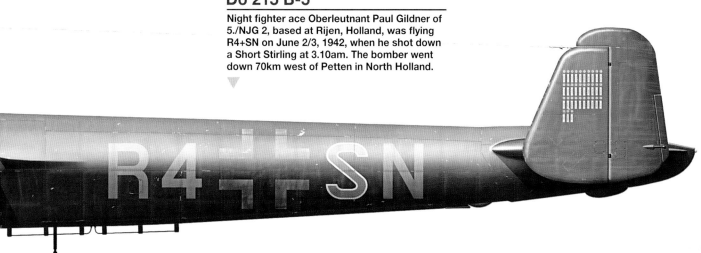

DORNIER DO 17/215/217

The first example, based on an E-2, was ready by February 1942. There were to be two versions of the Do 217 J: the J-1 fitted with the Spanner system and the J-2 with radar and four MG 151s instead of two MG FFs. The former was intended as a long-range 'intruder', prowling the skies over Britain, while the latter was intended for short range home defence. A total of 130 Do 217 Js were built between March and the end of December 1942, though it was criticized by crews for being too heavy and underpowered by its BMW 801 L engines.

The last Dornier night fighters were the Do 217 N-1 and N-2 – produced after the J. These had more powerful DB 603 A engines and came with Lichtenstein radar as standard equipment. The N-1 had extra fuel tanks fitted in its bomb bay and equipment for flying over water including a lifeboat and radio transmitters. Retaining the standard Do 217 bomb release gear, plus defensive machine gun positions in the upper and lower fuselage positions, it was heavy and slow, though 240 were built. The defensive gunnery positions could be deleted and faired over as the Do 217 N-1/U1 or a quartet of upward firing Schräge Musik MG 151 cannon could be fitted as the Do 217 N-1/U3.

The N-2 had the defensive positions deleted from the outset and it was lightened still further with the deletion of the bomb bay, bomb release mechanisms and even the openable bomb bay doors. Thanks to all this weight loss, armour protection for the crew could be increased and a total of 95 N-2s were built.

While Dornier's night fighters were always a compromise, and never particularly well liked by their crews, they were rapidly made available at a time when the Luftwaffe needed them most. ●

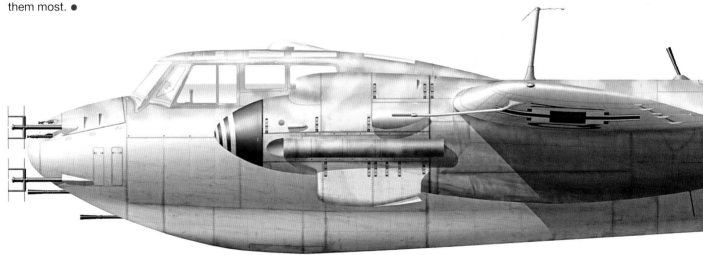

Do 217 N-2

A huge force of RAF bombers attacked railway yards and infrastructure around Paris on the night of May 1/2, 1944, and the fighters of 6./NJG 4 – operating the unpopular Do 217 N-2 – were among those sent to intercept them. Feldwebel Günther Konzack set off from Coulommiers in France in 3C+IP but hit bad weather and became disorientated. Well off course, he ended up flying in circles over Basel in neutral Switzerland. Eventually he landed, only to be surrounded and taken prisoner by Swiss soldiers – the aircraft being impounded.

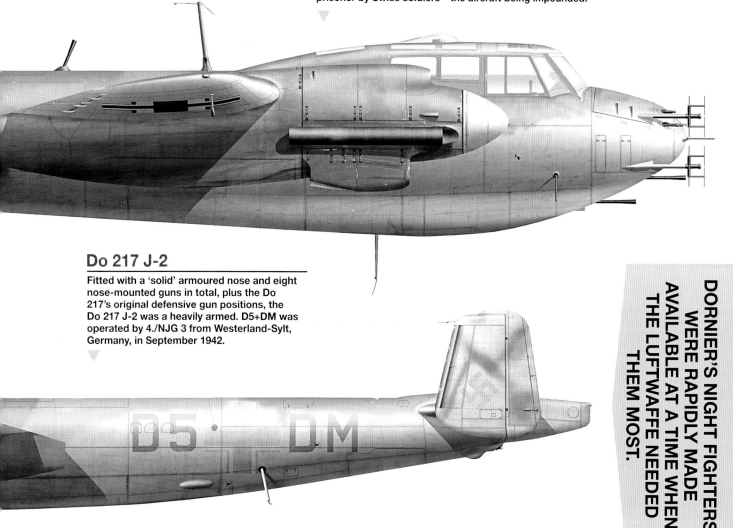

Do 217 J-2

Fitted with a 'solid' armoured nose and eight nose-mounted guns in total, plus the Do 217's original defensive gun positions, the Do 217 J-2 was a heavily armed. D5+DM was operated by 4./NJG 3 from Westerland-Sylt, Germany, in September 1942.

Do 217 N-2

The Do 217 N-2 was the final Dornier night fighter of the war but even this had been relegated to non-operational duties by the end of the war. SO+QY was serving with an unknown training unit stationed at Straubing in Germany when it was captured by the advancing Allied in May 1945.

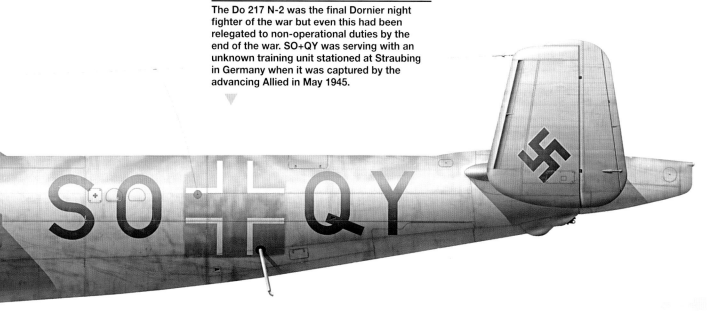

HEINKEL
HE 219

1942-1945

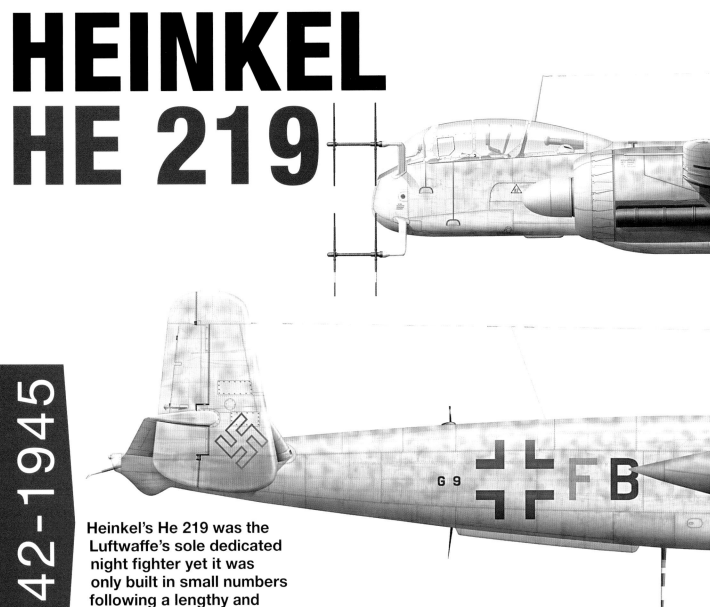

Heinkel's He 219 was the Luftwaffe's sole dedicated night fighter yet it was only built in small numbers following a lengthy and difficult development. Its pilots rated it highly, despite its unusual layout and insectoid looks.

W hat eventually became the He 219 started out as a single engine private venture reconnaissance machine presented to the Reichsluftfahrtministerium during April 1940. Heinkel was responding to a memo the ministry had put out bemoaning the Luftwaffe's lack of a good recce platform.

The RLM reaction was favourable and Heinkel continued to work on the project, designated P 1055, into 1941. The design eventually evolved into a heavy fighter under the new designation P 1056 – which was rejected

by the RLM in June 1941.

Heinkel refused to abandon the project, however, and at the end of 1941 the familiar twin-engine night fighter emerged as the P 1060. The commander of Germany's night fighter force, Generalleutnant Josef Kammhuber, took an interest in the project and the RLM ordered 12 prototypes of the aircraft under the new designation He 219 in January 1942.

Kammhuber himself inspected a mock-up on January 22 and the He 219 V1 prototype flew for the first time on November 6, 1942, powered by a pair of DB 603 A engines, and up to

January 15, 1943, made 46 flights. The use of DB 603 As, rather than the originally proposed DB 603 Gs, however, meant the aircraft was underpowered.

It also suffered from excessive tail vibration and poor lateral stability. Consequently a series of modifications were made and at the same time the V1 was fitted with four 30mm MK 108 cannon in a ventral weapons pack.

More prototypes were completed but a shortage of even DB 603 As delayed the construction of V7 and V8. In the meantime, Generalluftzeugmeister Erhard Milch had decided that

HE 219 A-0

Handley Page Halifax MZ310 disappeared without trace on the night of June 16/17, 1944. Hauptmann Paul Förster of Stab./NJG 1 based in Venlo, Holland, claimed the aircraft as a 'possible', stating that it went down in the North Sea 100km west of Amsterdam. He was flying G9+BA.

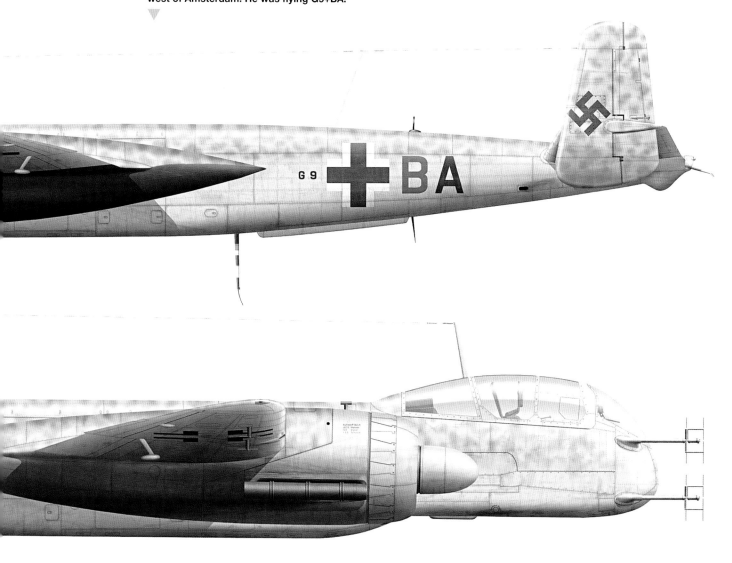

HE 219 V9

Flying He 219 V9 prototype G9+FB on the night of June 11/12, 1943, Major Werner Streib of Stab I./NJG 1, based at Venlo, Holland, claimed to have shot down five RAF bombers in just 30 minutes – instantly increasing the He 219's profile and its desirability. Unfortunately, he crashed on returning to base after his cockpit iced up and the V9's flaps failed to lock down. The aircraft was destroyed but Streib and his radar operator Helmut Fischer suffered only minor injuries.

producing the He 219 as a one-use type was a waste of valuable resources and made plans to cancel it in favour of the less specialized Junkers Ju 188.

Three competitors – the He 219 V1, Ju 188 E-1 and Dornier Do 217 were pitted against one another in a series of tests on March 25, 1943, with the conclusion that the He 219 outperformed both of its rivals. Milch argued that the Ju 188 should be the victor but the He 219 was ordered into production anyway, evidently on Kammhuber's authority.

The He 219 was flown into combat for the first time on the

night of June 11/12, 1943, and proved to be a great success. Serial production of the He 219 A-0 began on August 3, 1943, at Heinkel's Rostock-Marienehe factory, but only 30 examples had been completed by December 1. Deliveries to Luftwaffe units had commenced during October.

Powered by two DB 603 As, the A-0 was armed with a pair of MG 151/20s in its wing roots and either two or four cannon in the ventral weapons pack. Early examples were equipped with the FuG 212 Lichtenstein C-1 or C-2 radar unit. Later this was fitted in conjunction with the FuG 220,

then only the latter was installed.

Its engine nacelles were an integral part of the wing structure and the engines themselves drove three-bladed VDM variable pitch propellers which each had their own reservoir of de-icing fluid situated between the main and rear spars of the nacelle. In addition, the aircraft had no fewer than three heaters so that hot air could be directed internally to the areas most at risk of icing up.

Its tricycle undercarriage was hydraulically actuated and the wheel bay doors fully covered over the 840 x 300mm main wheels. In the event of a failure, the main

HEINKEL HE 219

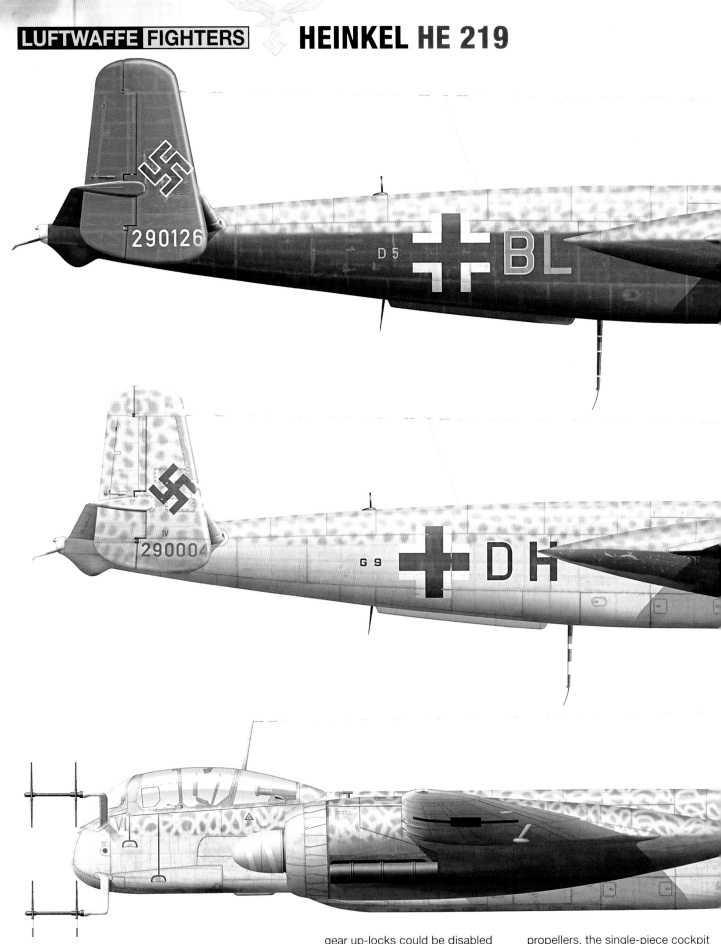

HE 219 A-7

Not many He 219s were built but this one, G9+HH, was still being operated by 1./NJG 1 from Westerland, Germany, right up to May 1945.

gear up-locks could be disabled and the wheels would swing down and lock into position under its own weight. The nosewheel emergency system locked it down using compressed air.

At the forward end of the fuselage, projecting ahead of the propellers, the single-piece cockpit was fastened on with bolts. The pilot and radar operator sat back-to-back on the world's first in-service ejection seat – which was necessary to ensure that neither crew member was caught by the propellers while trying to bail out.

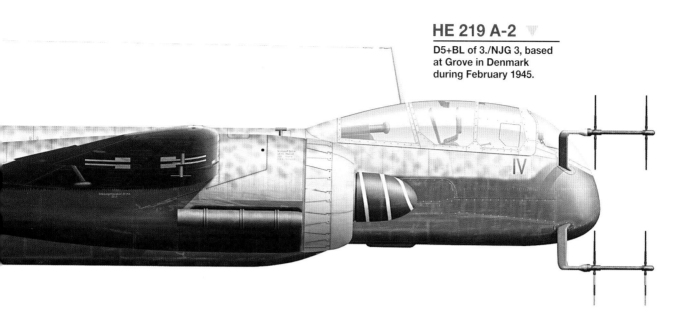

HE 219 A-2

D5+BL of 3./NJG 3, based at Grove in Denmark during February 1945.

HE 219 A-2

G9+DH was flown by pilots of 1./NJG 1. It wore this scheme at Paderborn, Germany, on April 10, 1945.

AFTER THE A-0 AND A-2 CAME THE A-7 AS THE LAST MAJOR PRODUCTION VERSION OF THE HE 219.

The glazed cockpit canopy was constructed in four sections and the windscreen had both its own spray and wiper. There was a ladder fitted on the port side beneath the cockpit, which swung down to allow the crew access.

While most German aircraft quickly moved beyond their pre-production A-0 variant, the He 219 never reached A-1, which would have involved the installation of a more streamlined canopy. Instead, some 104 A-0s were built up to November 30, 1944. It was built alongside the A-2 for a short while before this took over as the main production variant. The A-2 was similar to the A-0 but with additional armour plating, extra fuel capacity for extended range and flame dampers for its engines. Some 85 of these were manufactured. No A-3s or A-4s were built. It is believed that a handful of A-5 three-seater prototypes were made but it did not enter series production, and neither did the A-6. So after the A-0 and A-2 came the A-7 as the last major production version. An unknown number of these DB 603 E-powered machines, perhaps around 100, were built up to the end of the war.

A huge range of projected 'paper project' versions of the He 219 were drawn up but ultimately the type failed to make any real impact on the course of the war due to the small number produced.

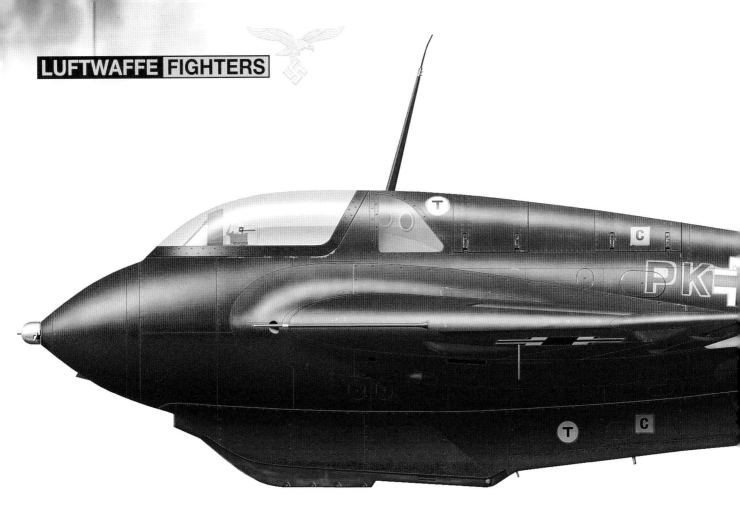

MESSERSCHMITT ME 163

Built in only tiny numbers, the rocket-propelled Me 163 was the product of a lengthy development programme and achieved little when it finally did reach the front line. However, its dramatic appearance in the skies over Germany stunned the Allies. Tales of impossibly fast bat-like fighters tearing through bombers with high-calibre cannon struck fear into the hearts of British and American aircrew and resulted in a string of improbable 'sightings'. Allied intelligence went into overdrive attempting to identify this new menace and work out ways of defending against it.

ircraft designer Alexander Lippisch, who had worked for the Zeppelin company after the First World War, began investigating the potential of tailless aerodynamic forms in 1921. By 1928, he was a director of the Research Institute of the Rhön-Rossitten Gesellschaft (RRG) – the world's first officially recognised glider school.

That year he was commissioned to build a rocket-powered glider by Max Valier and Friedrich Sander and during the years that followed he joined Die Deutsche Forschungsanstalt für Segelflug (DFS) – a major aviation research centre – and continued to work on tailless designs. In 1939, he left the DFS to work at Messerschmitt AG in Augsburg on a new design, the DFS 194, which would provide the basis for the Me 163 A rocket-powered prototype.

The design of the Me 163 A itself was finalised the following year and it made its first flight as a glider on February 13, 1941. Nearly six months later, on August 2, 1941, it flew for the first time under rocket power at Peenemunde. Two months after that, it was reaching speeds of 1000kph.

Following the successful tests of the early Me 163 A prototypes, the RLM placed an order for 70 Me 163 Bs, based on Lippisch's revised designs. Work on building the first prototype was started on December 1, 1941, but was delayed as Messerschmitt's resources were focused on other projects

Me 163 B V41

The Me 163's first combat sortie was flown by Major Wolfgang Späte of Erprobungskommando 16 from Bad Zwischenahn, Germany, on May 13, 1944. His aircraft PK+QL was painted red, either by the factory or his ground crew, to resemble Manfred von Richthofen's Fokker Dr.I.

notably the Me 262 and Me 264. Lippisch left the company in April 1943 and it was not until January 1944 that the first fully armed Me 163 B-0, V14, was delivered to the first Me 163 test squadron. The Luftwaffe received its first batch of full production model Me 163 B-1s in June 1944 and operations commenced in July 1944.

Me 163 flights were largely curtailed by fuel shortages but up to May 1945 the type was credited with 16 enemy aircraft destroyed – most of them bombers.

The B-1 was powered by a single Walter HWK 109-509 A-2 liquid-fuelled rocket engine, producing 3800lb of thrust. It was 5.98m long and 2.75m tall at the tip of its fin, with a wingspan of 9.33m. Its top speed was 596mph with a range of 25 miles and a service ceiling of 12,100m (39,700ft). Armament was a pair of 30mm MK 108 cannon.

The precise number of examples built may never be known but around five Me 163 prototypes were built, plus eight Me 163 A-0s, two Me 163 B prototypes, 30 pre-production B-0s and fewer than 400 B-1 production models. ●

UP TO MAY 1945 THE TYPE WAS CREDITED WITH 16 ENEMY AIRCRAFT DESTROYED – MOST OF THEM BOMBERS

Me 163 B-1

The first Me 163 victory was scored by Leutnant Hartmut Ryll of 1./JG 400 flying White 11 from Brandis in Germany on August 16, 1944. He destroyed a B-17 but was himself shot down and killed shortly afterwards. Two other Me 163 pilots also claimed B-17 'kills' during the same action.

Me 163 B-1

White 18 flown by Oberfeldwebel Wilhelm Josef 'Jupp' Mühlstroh of 2./JG 400, based at Brandis, Germany, during the spring of 1945.

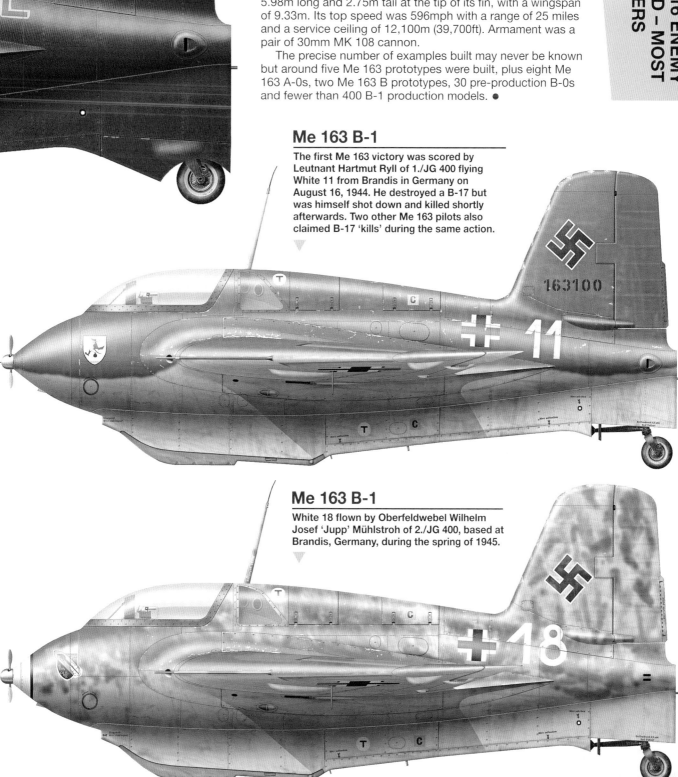

MESSERSCHMITT

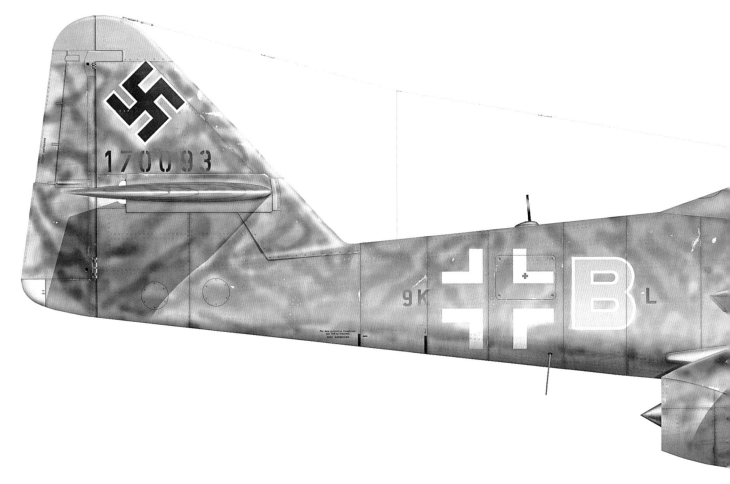

1939–1945

The world's first jet fighter and arguably the best fighter of the war overall, the Messerschmitt Me 262 was a deadly technological marvel with combat abilities that made it a legend in its own time. Conceived as a pure fighter but also produced in fighter-bomber and two-seater night fighter forms, the Me 262 underwent rapid development during its short front line career.

Even before the experimental Heinkel He 178 aircraft had proven that the principle of the jet engine was sound with its first flight on August 27, 1939, Heinkel and Messerschmitt were each given a development contract to create a fighter that would utilise the new powerplant.

Messerschmitt's project, the P 1065, was initially designed as a twin-boom aircraft similar to de Havilland's Vampire, then reshaped into something similar to the He 178 itself, with a nose intake. When it became clear that the power output of the first jet engines was likely to fall some way below initial projections, a twin-engine layout was adopted.

More detailed work to flesh out this basic form commenced on April 1, 1939, and an initial design featuring wings similar to those of the Me 109 was presented to the RLM for consideration on June 7, 1939. A mock-up was commissioned but the design continued to evolve and by the end of September the aircraft featured new enlarged wings. The first mock-up was inspected on December 19, 1939, but the changes kept coming, with swept-back wings appearing for the first time in a project description issued in February 1940.

A series of 20 prototypes each powered by a pair of BMW P 3302 engines was discussed on March 1, 1940. Although it was initially designed as a 'tail sitter', Willy Messerschmitt himself had penned versions of the P 1065 that featured a tricycle undercarriage.

The full production version of the aircraft was to be powered by the smaller BMW P 3304 and would carry an armament of three

ME 262

Me 262 A-2a

Hauptmann Hans-Christoph Buttmann of 3./KG 51 flew this Me 262 A-2a, coded 9K+BL, from Rheine in Germany on October 5, 1944 – the day he was killed. His aircraft crashed at Overasselt-Nederasselt in Holland.

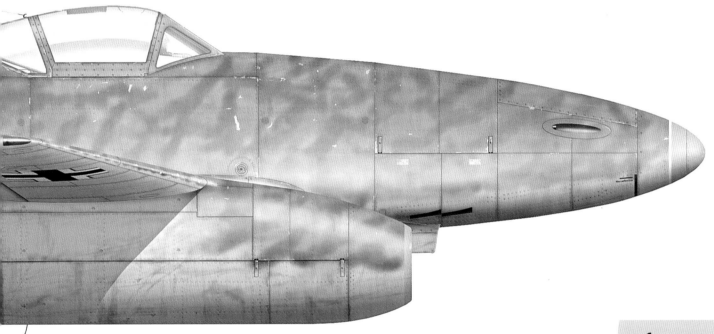

MG 151 20mm cannon in its nose. It would also boast advanced features such as an ejection seat, a pressure cabin and dive brakes. While it always seemed likely that the P 1065 would have its engines slung beneath its wings, wind tunnel tests where carried out on arrangements where the engines were mounted either centrally within the wings or even on top of them.

Despite early progress, it was clear by January 1941 that BMW was struggling to make either of its proposed engines production-ready and the situation was becoming increasingly desperate. Heinkel had already been tow-testing the engineless prototype of its design, the He 280, for four months by this point but the P 1065 did not even exist except on paper.

An alternative plan was hastily formulated – to build the P 1065 V1 and test it using a Jumo 210 G

piston engine fitted into its nose. This was approved and the P 1065 V1 was rapidly constructed between February and March 1941. It finally received the RLM designation Me 262 on April 8 and the Me 262 V1 flew for the first time using its piston engine on April 18. The He 280 V2 had flown using its twin HeS 8 jet engines three weeks earlier.

Eventually, two BMW P.3302 prototype engines were delivered to Messerschmitt in September 1941. In the meantime, the company had seriously considered fitting the Me 262 with three or four Argus As 014 pulse jet engines under each wing – just to get the project under way. On March 25, 1942, the Me 262 V1 took off for the first time using the pair of BMW P.3302s but almost immediately suffered compressor blade failure in both engines. Messerschmitt

was now looking further afield for an engine supplier.

Twenty pre-production Me 262s and five prototypes had been ordered on July 21, 1941, but in the light of this latest failure, on May 29, 1942, this was now reduced to just the prototypes. Three days later, a pair of Jumo 004 engines was delivered to Messerschmitt and within six weeks they had been fitted to the newly constructed Me 262 V3. On July 18, test pilot Fritz Wendel flew it for 12 minutes without problems in the morning, then again for another 13 minutes at around midday – reaching a top speed of 342mph.

More successful flights followed but on August 11 Rechlin test pilot Heinrich Beauvais crashed the V3 on take-off, causing substantial damage. Even so, the Me 262 V3's sustained success with its Jumo

MESSERSCHMITT SERIOUSLY CONSIDERED FITTING THE ME 262 WITH THREE OR FOUR ARGUS AS 014 PULSE JET ENGINES UNDER EACH WING – JUST TO GET THE PROJECT UNDER WAY

MESSERSCHMITT ME 262

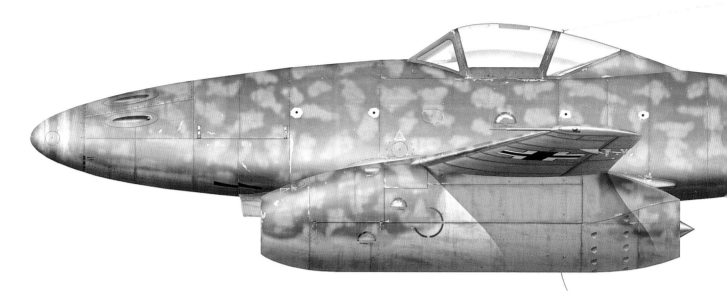

004s was the first real evidence that jet engines could be made to work successfully. The Me 262's series of pre-production aircraft was reinstated and it was quickly decided that Me 262 V2, which had been built for BMW P.3302 engines, should be converted to Jumo 004s by the end of September.

V3 was repaired and V4 and V5, also on Jumos, were scheduled for completion on January and March of 1943. Work on building V6 was set to commence in May 1943.

V2 flew with Jumo 004 engines twice on October 1, 1942, and the RLM increased its order to 30 pre-production aircraft – all of them now with tricycle undercarriages.

On March 4, 1943, a meeting was held to review the type's armament and it was decided that the originally proposed trio of MG 151 20mm cannon should be replaced with six MK 108 cannon

or two MK 108s and a pair of MG 151s. Five days later, and with news that a new lighter version of the Jumo 004 was nearing completion, the decision was taken to cancel Heinkel's He 280 and press ahead with the Me 262 as the Luftwaffe's first mass-produced jet fighter.

The Me 262 V2 was still the only version flying but it was joined on March 20 by the fully repaired V3 – just as well since V2 was completely destroyed in a crash during its 48th flight on April 18. V4 was completed on May 15, 1943.

With the He 280 out of the race, it now had to be decided whether to build the Me 209 in quantity to replace the Me 109 or to put the Me 262 onto production lines instead. The Me 209 was an evolution of the Me 109 but featuring a

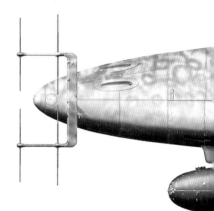

larger fuselage and wide-track undercarriage. The decision was down to Erhard Milch and in order to help him make up his mind he asked his trusted friend and colleague Adolf Galland, General of Fighters, to evaluate the Me 262.

Me 262 A-1a

Yellow 8 of 3./JG 7 as it appeared at Stendal in Germany on April 15, 1945, shortly after being captured by US forces.

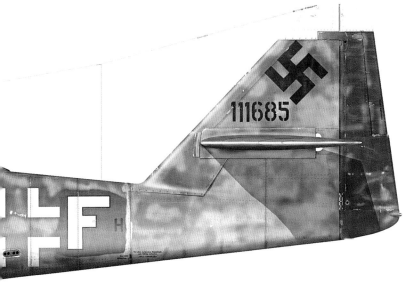

Me 262 A-2a

This Me 262 A-2a, 9K+FH belonging to 1./KG 51, was abandoned as unserviceable at Brunnthal, Germany, in early May 1945.

Me 262 B-1a/U1

Red 12, WNr.111980, of 10./NJG 11 was flown by Leutnant Herbert Altner from Magdeburg, Germany, on April 6, 1945. Altner survived the war with 24 night and one day victories having served with NJG 3, NJG 5 and NJG 11.

Galland test-flew the Me 262 V4 on May 22, 1943, and quickly became the type's most ardent and influential supporter. He famously reported to Reichsmarschall Hermann Göring that: "It flies as if there is an angel pushing." Nine days later, Göring officially declared that production of the Me 209 was to be suspended in favour of the Me 262.

Me 262 V5, the first prototype to be fitted with a tricycle undercarriage, first flew on June 6, 1943, and demonstrated a marked improvement in take-off performance compared to the earlier 'tail dragger' versions.

Me 262 V6 was the first Me 262 prototype to be fitted with a fully retractable tricycle undercarriage, and it made its first flight on October 17, 1943.

V6 was also armed with a trio of MG 151s, and was powered by the Jumo 004B – a jet engine similar in size and shape to its 004A predecessor but weighing 240lb less – a combined saving across the two engines of 480lb.

On October 27, 1943, Hitler emphasised the role he envisioned the Me 262 playing during the long-anticipated Allied invasion of France. He said: "The jet fighter with bombs will be vital, because at the given moment it will scream at top speed along the beaches and hurl its bombs into the massive build-up that is bound to be there."

GALLAND TOLD GÖRING: "IT FLIES AS IF THERE IS AN ANGEL PUSHING."

MESSERSCHMITT ME 262

Then at a display of the Luftwaffe's latest experimental equipment on November 26 at Insterburg airfield, East Prussia, Hitler went to inspect the two Me 262s on show – V1 and V6. Indicating them, he said: "I'm not interested in this aircraft as a fighter. Can it carry bombs?"

Willy Messerschmitt assured him that it could – one 1000kg bomb or two 500kg bombs. Hitler then said: "At last, this is the aircraft I have been demanding for years. Here it is, but nobody recognised it. I order this aircraft be built as a bomber."

The Me 262 V7 first flew on December 20, 1943, with all the same innovations as the V6 but with the addition of a rubber-sealed pressure cabin. It was followed by the

V9 on January 19, 1944, which was used to test the new bubble cockpit canopy and radio and electrical equipment.

V8 was completed on March 18 and was to be the A-series production prototype. In most respects it was similar to the V9 but had a quartet of MK 108 30mm cannon in the nose – what was to soon become the well-known standard armament of the Me 262 A-1a.

Serial production slowly commenced in April 1944 with the Me 262 being equipped as a fighter. Strenuous efforts were made, however, to work out how the aircraft could be made to carry a useful bomb load since Hitler was adamant that it should operate as a fast bomber during the Allied invasions he knew were imminent.

Some standard A-1a aircraft were modified to carry two ETC 503 bomb racks under their fuselage, ahead of the main landing gear wheel wells, and a load of one SC 250, two SC 250s, one SC 500 or one SD 500.

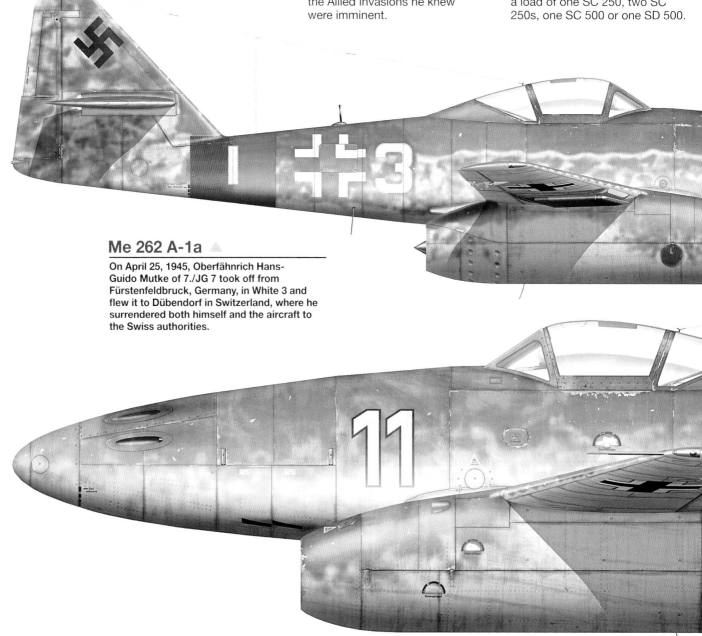

Me 262 A-1a

On April 25, 1945, Oberfähnrich Hans-Guido Mutke of 7./JG 7 took off from Fürstenfeldbruck, Germany, in White 3 and flew it to Dübendorf in Switzerland, where he surrendered both himself and the aircraft to the Swiss authorities.

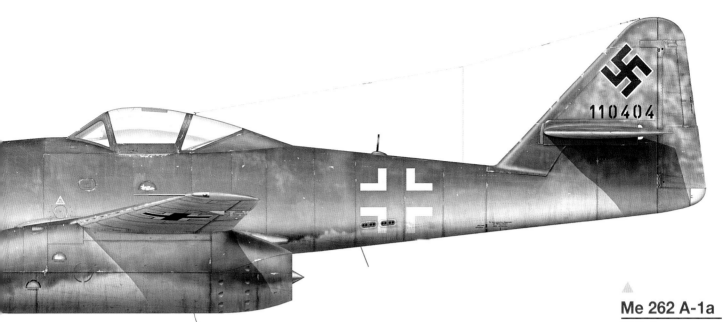

Within a short time however, a new variant, the Me 262 A-2a, was devised. This saw the standard A-1a's two upper MK 108 cannon removed and electrical arming and release systems fitted.

Proposals for a Me 262 night fighter with two seats and radar equipment were drawn up shortly

before September 1, 1944. The aircraft was to be based on the trainer version of the type, which already had two seats.

The dual controls were to be removed and replaced with two new 140 litre fuel tanks, one on either side of the rear seat. This would give the aircraft a total fuel capacity of 2070 litres – with the option of adding two 300 litre drop tanks externally and another 900 litres in a winged fuel tank that could be towed behind the aircraft.

The rear position was to be occupied by a FuG 218 Neptun

V airborne interception radar and its operator. It was intended that a FuG 350 Zc Naxos homing device should also be fitted.

Design work on the Me 262 night fighter, known today but possibly not at the time as the Me 262 B-1a/U1, progressed rapidly and by late January or early February 1945 work began on creating the first examples at the Berlin-Staaken workshops of Deutsche Lufthansa.

A number of Lechfeld-built Me 262 A-1as were delivered to the facility and underwent significant

Me 262 A-1a

White 1 was flown by Leutnant Franz Schall of Kommando Nowotny from Achmer in Germany during October 1944. Schall was the war's third highest scorer of jet victories. His overall tally of 133 included, while flying the Me 262, six four-engined bombers and 10 P-51 Mustangs. He was killed on April 10, 1945.

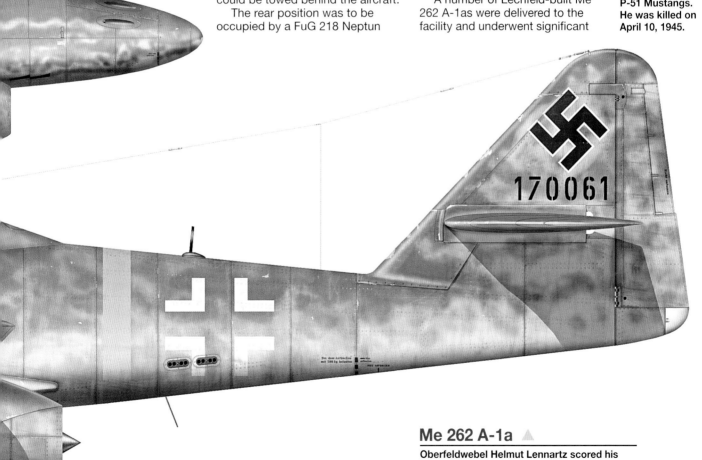

Me 262 A-1a

Oberfeldwebel Helmut Lennartz scored his first aerial victory – a Boeing B-17 Flying Fortress – while flying this aircraft, White 11 of Erprobungskommando 262, from Lechfeld in Germany on August 15, 1944.

MESSERSCHMITT ME 262

Me 262 A-1a ▶

Red 13 of III./EJG 2 was flown by Major Heinz Bär from Lechfeld in Germany on March 19, 1945 – the day he scored his first jet victory, shooting down a P-51 Mustang.

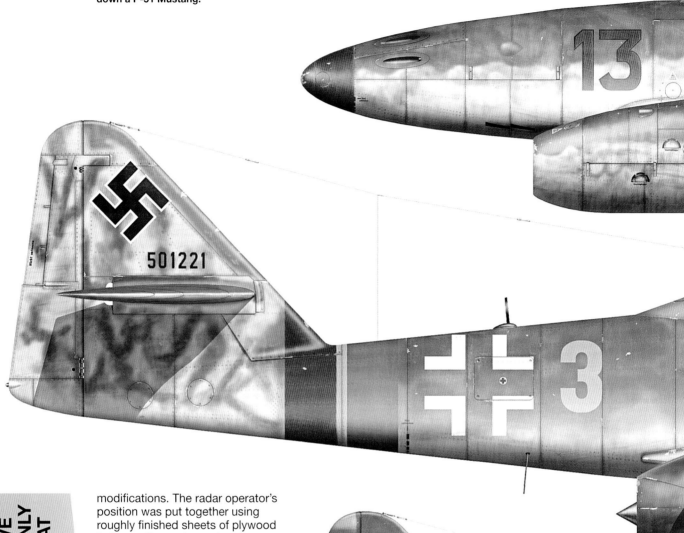

OVERALL, SOME 1443 ME 262S ARE KNOWN TO HAVE BEEN COMPLETED, BUT ONLY AROUND 300 SAW COMBAT

modifications. The radar operator's position was put together using roughly finished sheets of plywood to house the equipment and instruments but it is unlikely that the Naxos device was ever fitted to any of the small number of examples built – most likely between six and 12.

While the Luftwaffe waited for the first deliveries of its first jet-powered night fighter, a unit was set up by night fighter ace Leutnant Kurt Welter to test the standard Me 262A-1a during the hours of darkness. Based at Rechlin-Lärz, Kommando Welter flew a series of night interception missions against RAF aircraft from November 2, 1944, into early 1945.

The unit was redesignated 10./NJG 11 on January 25, 1945. It received its first Me 262 B-1a/U1 on March 22 and only four of these aircraft are known to have seen action before the war ended.

Overall, some 1443 Me 262s are known to have been completed, but only around 300 saw combat. ●

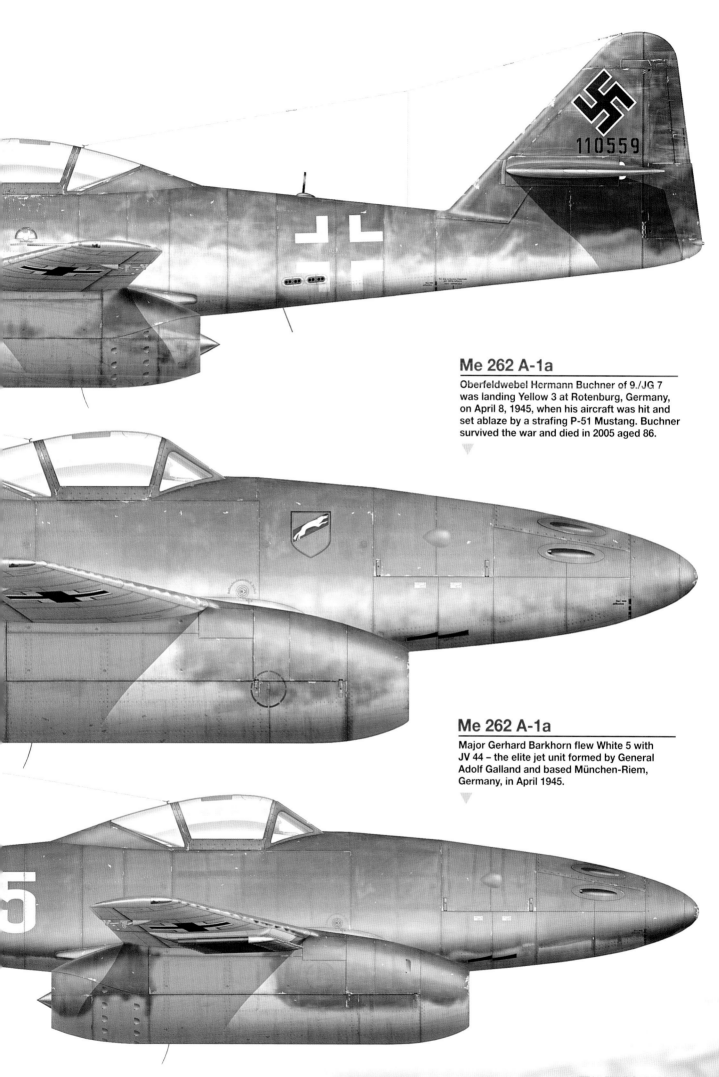

Me 262 A-1a

Oberfeldwebel Hermann Buchner of 9./JG 7 was landing Yellow 3 at Rotenburg, Germany, on April 8, 1945, when his aircraft was hit and set ablaze by a strafing P-51 Mustang. Buchner survived the war and died in 2005 aged 86.

Me 262 A-1a

Major Gerhard Barkhorn flew White 5 with JV 44 – the elite jet unit formed by General Adolf Galland and based München-Riem, Germany, in April 1945.

He 162 A-2

Yellow 21 of 3./JG 1, based at Leck,
Germany, in May 1945.

HEINKEL HE 162

1944-1945

The last Luftwaffe aircraft to enter service during the Second World War, the Heinkel He 162 Volksjäger was born out of desperation. Originally intended as a cheap jet fighter that even novice pilots could take into combat without difficulty, it was rushed into production as the war entered its final phase. The end result was a flawed little aircraft that was anything but easy to fly.

A requirement for a new single jet engine fighter for the Luftwaffe was issued on September 10, 1944.

It called for a straightforward design using wood and steel as much as possible, and powered by the weak but well developed BMW 003 engine. This Volksjäger or people's fighter was to be simple to build and easy to fly too.

Trained and experienced pilots were in increasingly short supply by this time and it was hoped that even raw recruits would be able to fly the new fighter without difficulty.

Arado, Blohm & Voss, Fieseler, Focke-Wulf, Heinkel, Junkers, Messerschmitt and Siebel were all invited to participate but given only four days to put together their

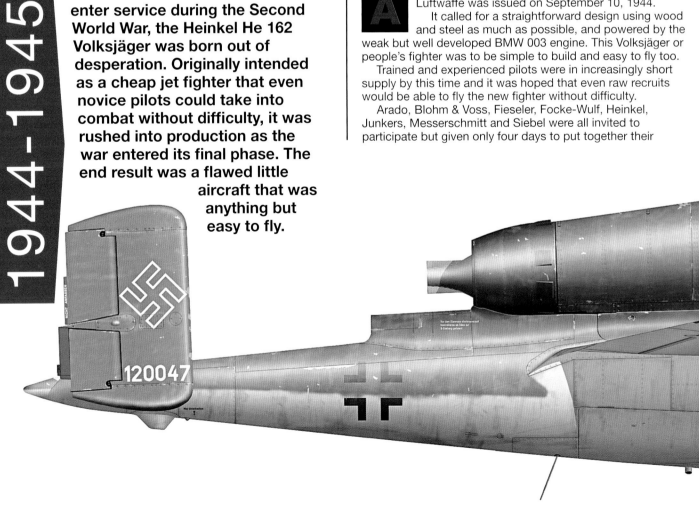

120047

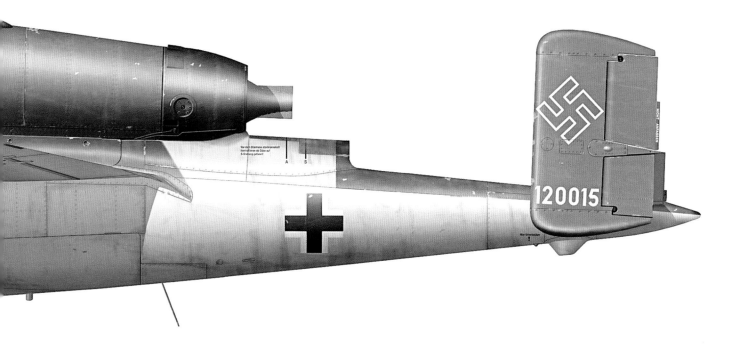

proposals. Messerschmitt was strongly opposed to this new competition and refused to tender, while Fieseler and Siebel were simply incapable of meeting the deadline.

The designs put forward by Arado, Blohm & Voss, Focke-Wulf and Junkers were rapidly assessed and dismissed, leaving the Heinkel P 1073 as the winner. Hitler ordered it into mass production as the He 162 on September 23.

Rather than complete all the design drawings first, then begin building tools and jigs in the usual way, the first metal was cut for the initial He 162 prototypes on October 25, 1944, even as the designers and engineers continued their work.

Two basic variants were envisioned – the He 162 A-1 armed with a pair of 30mm MK 108 cannon – and the A-2 fitted with two MG 151/20s. The undercarriage was based on parts borrowed from the Me 109 and Heinkel decided to fit the same ejection seat as that used on the He 219.

Just two months and three weeks after the design specification was announced, on December 1, the He 162 M1 (V1) was completed. It was first flown on December 6 but during another test, four days later, the leading edge of its

starboard wing came off and it crashed, killing test pilot Gotthold Peter.

He 162 M2, the second prototype, made its maiden flight on December 22 and eight more prototype and pre-production aircraft were rapidly completed thereafter. At the same time, even as testing got under way in earnest, Heinkel was already gearing up its factories to begin full series production – aiming to produce a quota of 30 He 162 A-1 aircraft by January 31, 1945.

JG 1 was chosen as the first unit to convert to the He 162. I./JG 1 was pulled back from the front line on February 6 for this purpose and transferred to Parchim, 50 miles south of Rostock, on February 9. No He 162s were immediately available, so I./JG 1's pilots and crew began familiarisation training with Heinkel personnel on February 12.

THE HE 162 M1 (V1) FIRST FLEW ON DECEMBER 6, 1944, BUT DURING ANOTHER TEST THE LEADING EDGE OF ITS WING CAME OFF AND IT CRASHED, KILLING ITS PILOT

He 162 A-2
White 4 of 1./JG 1, flown by Major Werner Zober, Leck, Germany, May 5, 1945.

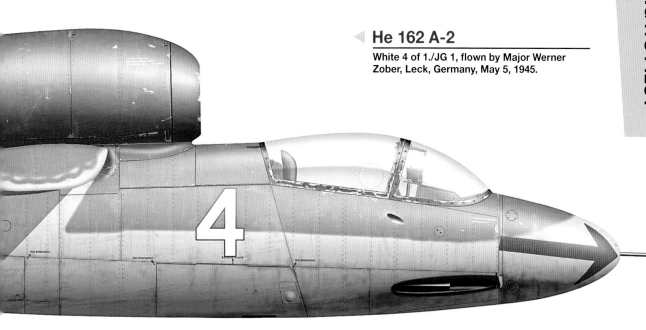

HEINKEL HE 162

An Auffangsstaffel or 'collection squadron' from 2./JG 1 was sent to Heinkel's Rostock headquarters on February 27 to pick up a single aircraft brought over from Junkers at Bernburg – He 162 M19 WNr. 220002. A second group of pilots arrived at Rostock on March 4 to collect more aircraft but none were available.

He 162 M19 was destroyed in a fatal crash on March 14, leaving the pilots once again without a single working example for conversion training. On March 26, it was announced that JG 1 would relocate in readiness to receive completed aircraft leaving the Junkers production line. A group of 15 pilots from 3./JG 1 moved to Lechfeld but there was still nothing available to fly.

I./JG 1 was told on March 31 that it would have to move to Leck at the northernmost extreme of Germany. On the same day, with JG 1 personnel now scattered across Germany, He 162 deliveries finally began.

By April 12, 1945, I./JG 1 had 16 He 162s at Parchim, of which 10-12 were serviceable.

The He 162 was approaching true front line service when the war ended. Heinkel's Rostock production facility was overrun on or shortly after May 1.

It is believed that, in the end, some 171 He 162s were built, with 116 actually being delivered. The Luftwaffe received 56 of these before production finally collapsed at the end of April. ●

He 162 A-2

An unusual starboard side view of Red 1 flown by Leutnant Gerhard Hanf of Leck-based 2./JG 1. On the port side, ground crew painted the word 'Nervenklau' in late April 1945, apparently in recognition of the fact that the sound of his motorcycle's engine got on their nerves as he rode it to the airfield.

He 162 A-2

Leutnant Rudolf Schmitt of 1./JG 1 was flying White 1 when he allegedly shot down an RAF Typhoon near Rostock on May 4, 1945 – the only 'kill' claimed for the He 162 during the war.

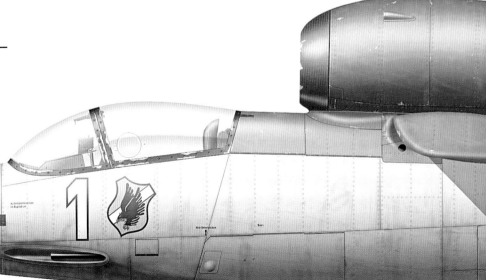

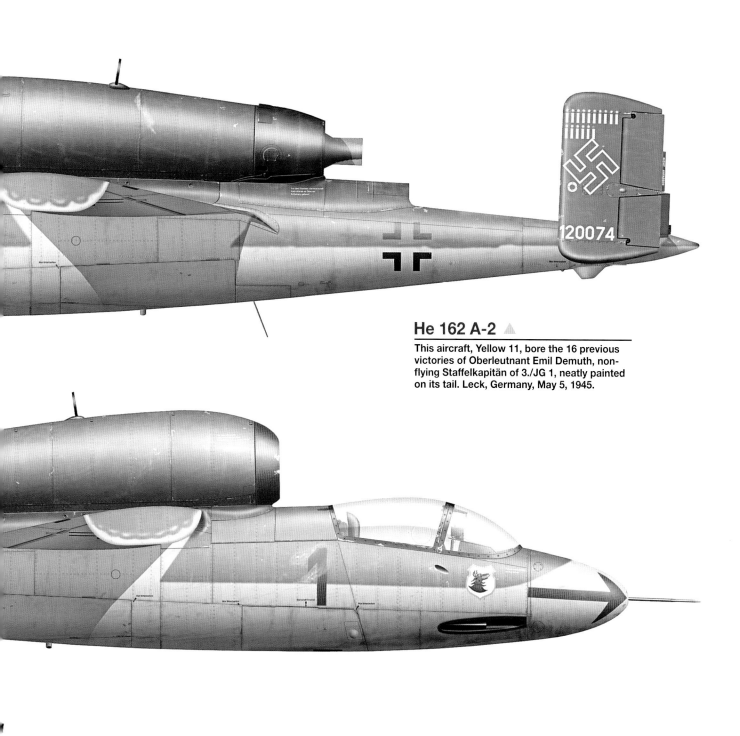

He 162 A-2

This aircraft, Yellow 11, bore the 16 previous victories of Oberleutnant Emil Demuth, non-flying Staffelkapitän of 3./JG 1, neatly painted on its tail. Leck, Germany, May 5, 1945.

COLOUR CHART

RLM 65 1939	RLM 65 1941
RLM 70	RLM 71	RLM 74 VARIANT	RLM 74 VARIANT
RLM 75 VARIANT	RLM 75 VARIANT	RLM 76 1941	RLM 76 1944/45
RLM 76 LATE WAR	RLM 76 LATE WAR	RLM 78	RLM 79
RLM 80	RLM 81 VARIANT	RLM 81 VARIANT	RLM 81 VARIANT
RLM 81 VARIANT	RLM 82 VARIANT	RLM 82 VARIANT	RLM 83